Photoshop IQ

First Edition 1995
Published in the United States of America by

Silver Pixel Press
Division of The Saunders Group
21 Jet View Drive
Rochester, NY 14624
Fax: (716) 328-5078

From the German Edition by
Dieter K. Froebish, Holger Lindner and Thomas Steffen
English text by James Wondrack
Translated by Hayley Ohlig

ISBN 1-883403-25-1

Photoshop IQ

Imaging Effects for MAC & PC

Dieter K. Froebisch · Holger Lindner · Thomas Steffen · James Wondrack

Contents

Screening

Screen Structures

Solarizations

Colorizations

Dynamic Effects

Montages and Masks

Drawing Techniques

ILLUSTRATIONS

Introduction

As personal computers and off-the-shelf software become increasingly accessible and powerful, more digital possibilities are available to the public. Personal computers, along with software programs like Adobe Photoshop™, have become the center of the creative imaging world. Because of this, lines are being blurred between traditional roles within the creative community. These changes are unsettling to some, but for those who take advantage of this new generation of imaging, it means opportunity.

Keep in mind the computer is only a tool, and the cognitive process of creating will never change. As with any medium, in order to realize the potential, the process must first be mastered. Along with the new process comes a learning curve. This book is designed to help shorten that curve through its unique approach to learning Adobe Photoshop. It takes the user immediately into the working environment of digital image manipulation through the age-old method of "learning by seeing and doing."

This compendium illustrates more than 110 image manipulation techniques, ranging from basic screening to complex montaging. These are presented as "recipes," with the resultant image on the opposite page. The recipes are designed to get you up and running, to provide a quick reference for a variety of techniques and as a source of inspiration for your own creative endeavors.

Preface

The concept for this book grew out of an earlier study in traditional photographic design techniques. In place of classic, chemical-based photography, examples are used from the "digital photo lab." All effects are applied to the same scanned photograph so you can easily make a visual analysis of how the manipulation affects the end result. It also makes it easy to perceive the actual effect without getting "lost" in the image and thus, easier to judge if the raw effect is appropriate for another application.

Throughout this book, we have modified a single image into more than 110 black-and-white or color images to illustrate the infinite possibilities of computer image manipulation. The final images represent the framework of image manipulation – from rudimentary screens to complex multi-step montages. The procedures are further illustrated with screen shots of the actual dialog boxes that correspond to a particular instruction.

An examination of all possible forms of manipulation would be impossible to address in one volume. However, this book takes focuses on exhibiting many of the building blocks essential to the creative professional.

As you progress, you will not only think of *Photoshop IQ* as instructional, but also as a source book that unveils the infinite possibilities of digital imaging.

Prerequisites

This book is intended to enhance your creativity with digital image manipulation and with Adobe Photoshop in particular. Before beginning, you should have a working knowledge of your operating system's conventions (presumably Macintosh System 7.x or Microsoft Windows 3.x™) and Adobe Photoshop version 3.0.1 or greater.

How you set up your machine can greatly affect your system's performance. Make sure your setup meets or exceeds that of the software manufacturer's recommendations. As a general rule in regards to system configuration, the more physical RAM (Random Access Memory) you have installed the better. Memory cheaters like RAM Doubler™ or Apple's Virtual Memory™ are not particularly effective with Photoshop. For best results, allocate a sufficient amount of memory (3 to 5 times the amount of your file's size) to Photoshop. Designating a "scratch disk" will also help performance. Monitor setup and calibration are also vital. Consult the Adobe Photoshop manual for further details.

Technical Data

▶ *File available online:*

A graphics file of the original image of the eye used in *Photoshop IQ* can be downloaded from the Photography Forums on America Online and CompuServe.

Description: Photoshop IQ

▶ *Original for all subjects:*

Black-and-white photographic print measuring 6.5 x 6 inches (170 x 155mm)

▶ *Scan resolution:*

300 dots per inch (dpi) at a ratio of 1:1

▶ *Computer hardware and software:*

■ Apple Macintosh IIfx with 20Mb of RAM and a 200Mb hard drive

■ UMAX 600 Flatbed desktop scanner

■ Scanning software: Cirrus 1.5 (available in Europe)

■ Image manipulation program: Adobe Photoshop 2.5.1 and 3.0.1

■ Drawing software: Aldus FreeHand 3.1

▶ *Output hardware:*

All images were imported into Pagemaker 5.0 and output at 2400 dpi through a Postscript RIP 9000 PS to a Compugraphic 9400 imagesetter.

▶ *Printing resolution:*

150 lines per inch (lpi) with an elliptical dot.

▶ *The following rules regarding image resolution should be taken into consideration:*

The greater the dimensions and resolution, the more memory an image file demands (both RAM and storage). Set image resolution 1.5 to 2 times the final line screen at 1:1. This book was printed at 150 line screen, therefore this book's halftones were set to 220 dpi. It's important when applying effects to work in the determined resolution (or greater) at all times in order to maintain the image's integrity. Interpolating, or increasing the resolution, will degrade the image. When combining halftone images with line art, work in 300 dpi.

Platform Differences

Adobe intelligently designed Photoshop to operate in all platforms. However, shortcuts and alternate functions are performed using different keystrokes. To simplify instructions, Macintosh commands are used in the text. The chart below lists the key equivalents for other platforms.

Macintosh	Windows	SGI Default System	SGI New System
Shift	Shift	Shift	Shift
Command (⌘)	Control	Control	Alt
Option	Alt	Alt	Ctrl_L
Control	None	None	Ctrl_R

Data Panel

Layout Program	Resolution:	**300** dpi
✓ Scan Program	Size:	14 MB
✓ Graphics Program	Difficulty:	▨▨
☑ Digital Imaging		▲

This data panel appears at the top of each text page to provide basic information about software and system requirements. On the left, the type of program used to create the image is indicated by a black box with a check. Programs with plain check marks are alternative choices. On the right, image resolution, image file size, and difficulty (simple, intermediate or complex) are indicated.

Adobe Photoshop 3.0 Toolbox

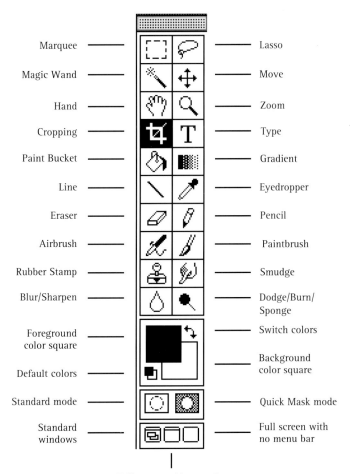

Marquee — Lasso
Magic Wand — Move
Hand — Zoom
Cropping — Type
Paint Bucket — Gradient
Line — Eyedropper
Eraser — Pencil
Airbrush — Paintbrush
Rubber Stamp — Smudge
Blur/Sharpen — Dodge/Burn/Sponge
Foreground color square — Switch colors
Default colors — Background color square
Standard mode — Quick Mask mode
Standard windows — Full screen with no menu bar

Full screen with menu bar

BASIC TECHNIQUES

Basic Photoshop techniques should not be underestimated. Not only are they the basis for creating more complex manipulated images, they themselves are often the best solution. The initial halftone, line art and posterization techniques discussed in this chapter are merely an introduction to the possibilities of Adobe Photoshop.

Halftone Image

This image serves as the subject or original halftone to which modifications are applied throughout this book.

- The image's value depth and range were adjusted using the Brightness/Contrast controls of the scanning software. The output device and monitor must be calibrated in order for the image on the screen to match the hardcopy output.

▶*Page 11 (Chapter Title Page): Negative Halftone*
Open the original halftone in Photoshop. (⌘O or **File***)*
Invert the image. (⌘I or **Image>Map***)*

▶*Page 14: Decreased Contrast*
Adjust the tonal range of the image.
Open the original halftone in Photoshop. (⌘O or **File***)*
Open the Brightness/Contrast dialog box. (⌘B or **Image>Adjust***)*
Drag the contrast sliders to the left to decrease the contrast level.

▶*Page 15: Increased Contrast*
Open the original halftone in Photoshop. (⌘O or **File***)*
Open the Brightness/Contrast dialog box. (⌘B or **Image>Adjust***)* 1
Drag the Contrast slider to the right to increase the contrast level.

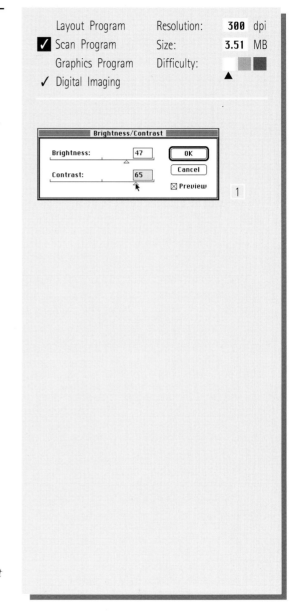

Layout Program | Resolution: | **300** dpi
☑ Scan Program | Size: | **3.51** MB
Graphics Program | Difficulty:
✓ Digital Imaging

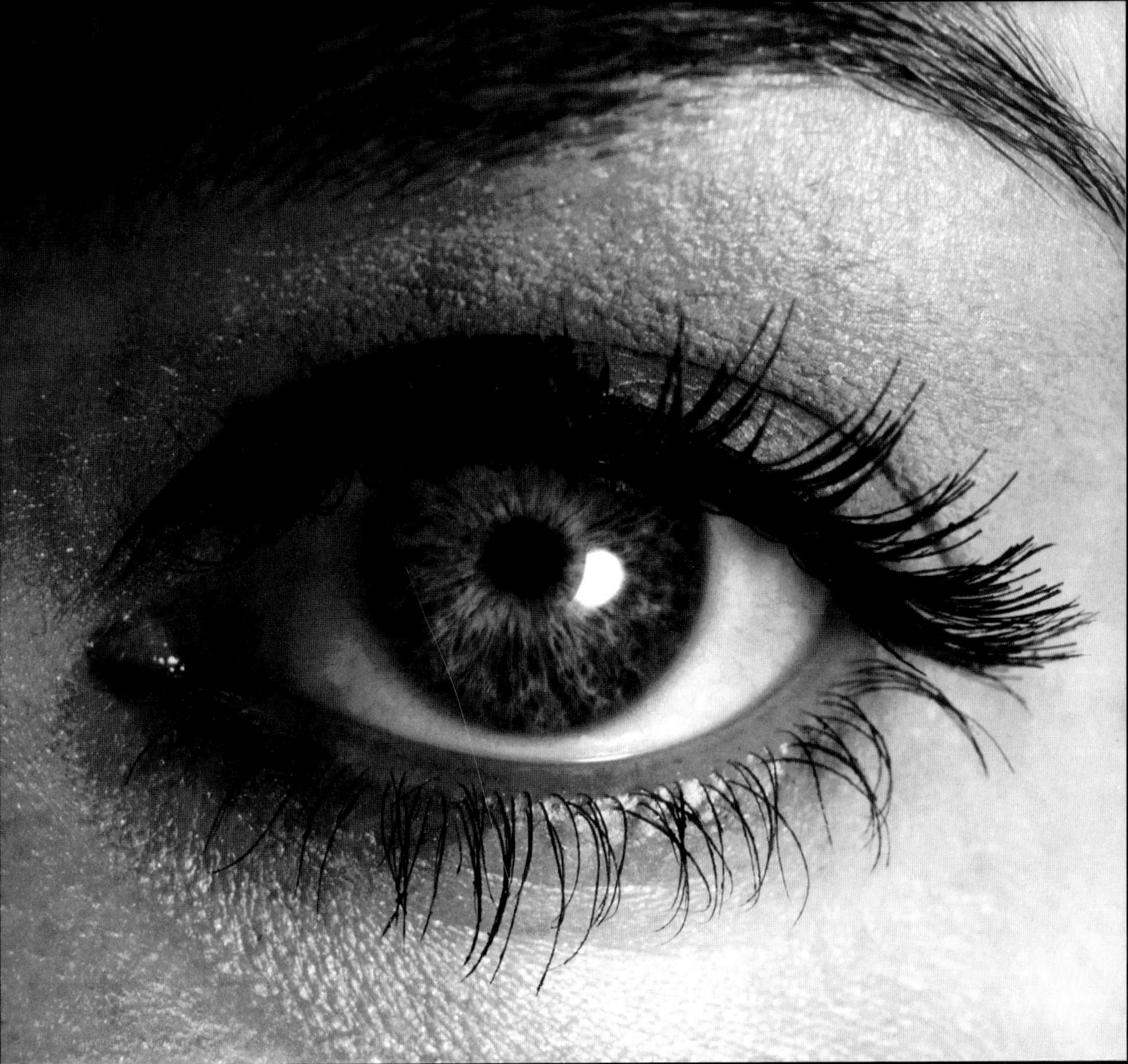

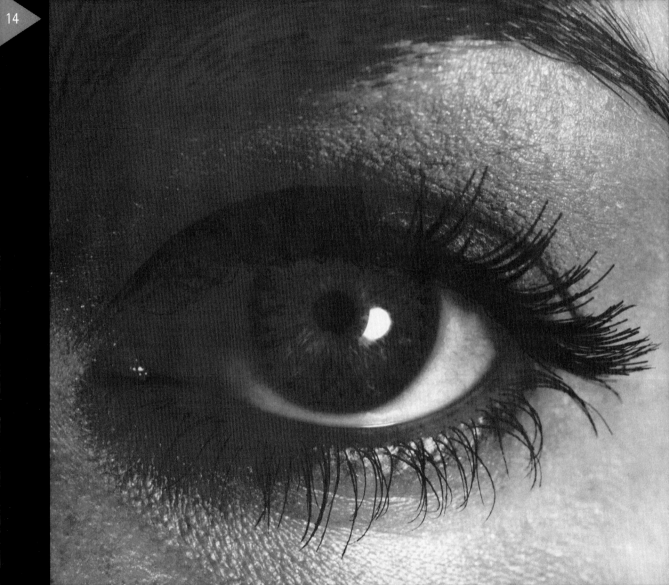

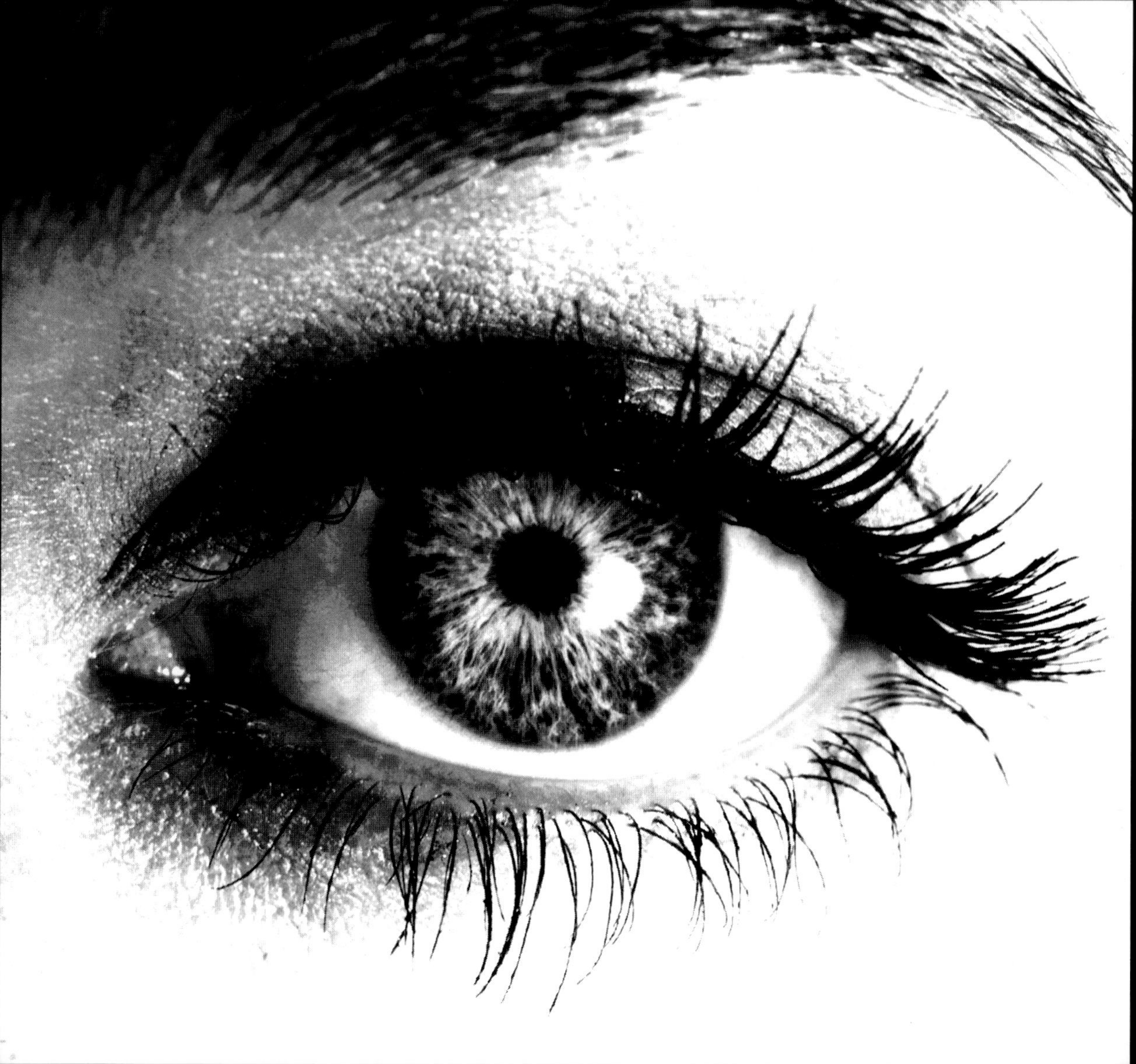

Line Art Conversion

✓ Layout Program   Resolution: **300** dpi
✓ Scan Program   Size: **3.7** MB
✓ Graphics Program   Difficulty:
☑ Digital Imaging

- Open the original halftone in Photoshop. (⌘**O** or **File**)

- Set the image threshold:
  Open the Threshold dialog box. (⌘**T** or **Image>Map**) 1
     Threshold Level: 50

The value represents the level in which tones are either converted to black or white. Pixels greater than the threshold change to white. Pixels less than the threshold change to black.

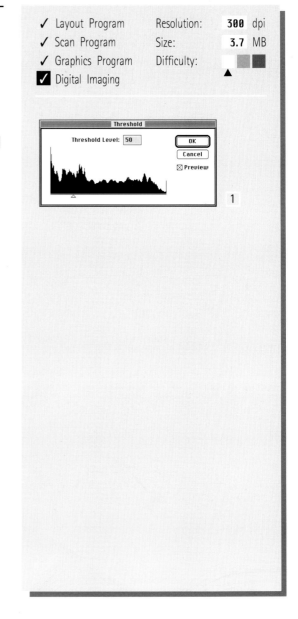

Pictogram

Convert the grayscale image to a high-contrast black-and-white image ready to be converted into a vector-based image used by drawing programs such as FreeHand or Adobe Illustrator.

- Open the original halftone in Photoshop. (⌘O or **File**)

- Open the Brightness/Contrast dialog box. (⌘B or **Image>Adjust**) 1
  Brightness: 50   Contrast: 100

- Choose Image Size. (**Image**) 2
  Constrain: Proportions
  Resolution: 600 pixels/inch
  Click OK. *The image will be increased to 600 dpi.*

- Apply the Gaussian Blur filter. (**Filter>Blur**) 3
  Radius: 40 pixels

- Open the Levels dialog box. (⌘L or **Image>Adjust**) 4
  Input levels:
  Black: 130   Gamma: 1.00   White: 141

- Select the Bitmap mode option. (**Mode**)
  Output: 600 pixels/inch
  Method: 50% Threshold
  Click OK. *This is will reduce the file's storage requirements while maintaining high resolution.*

- Save the image as a TIFF. (**File**)
  It will be utilized on Page 32.

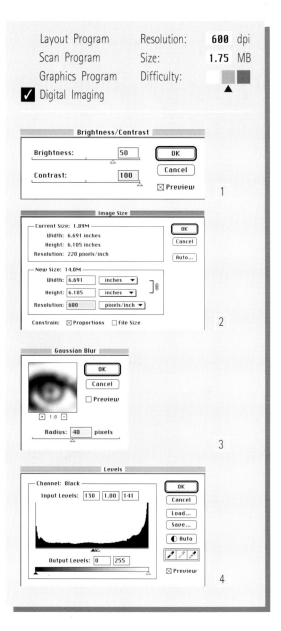

Layout Program   Resolution: **600** dpi
Scan Program   Size: **1.75** MB
Graphics Program   Difficulty:
✔ Digital Imaging

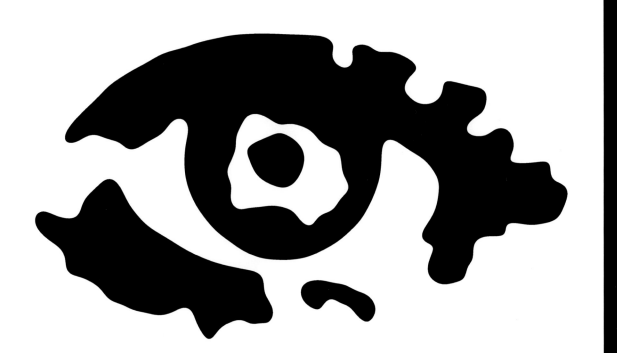

Posterize

- Open the original halftone in Photoshop. (**⌘O** or **File**)

- Open the Posterize dialog box. (**Image>Map**) 1
    Levels: 3
    Click OK. *The image will be reduced to three tones.*

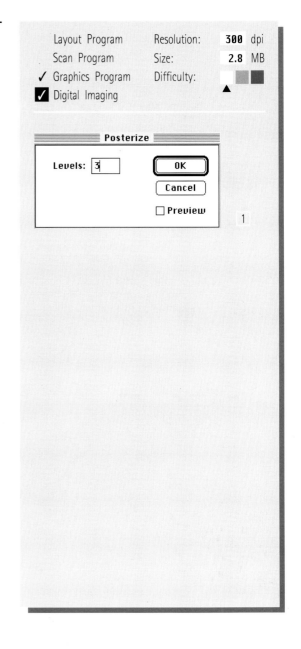

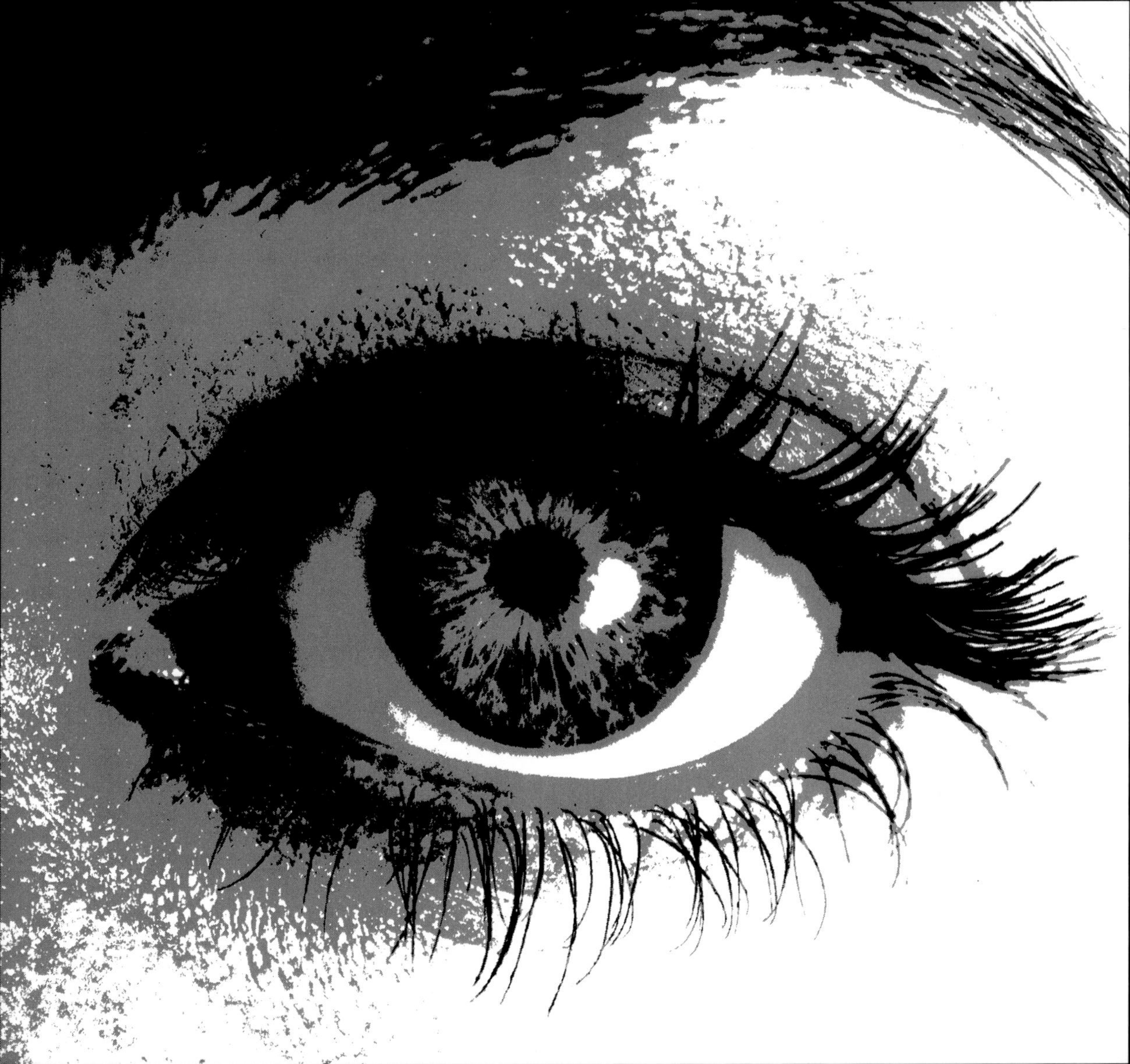

Color Posterization

Execute a four level Posterization, and assign custom color values.

- Open the original halftone in Photoshop. (⌘0 or **File**)

- Select the RGB mode option. (**Mode**)
  Select the Indexed Colors mode option. (**Mode**)

- Open the Posterize dialog box. (**Image>Map**) 1
    Levels: 4

- Open the Color Table dialog box. (**Mode**) 2
      Table: Custom
  Select an entire group of squares (values) from a single tonal range. This will automatically bring up the Color Picker. Choose a first color and a last color from the Color Picker. *Photoshop creates a gradient ranging between the first and last color chosen.*

- Repeat this procedure for all remaining gray levels.

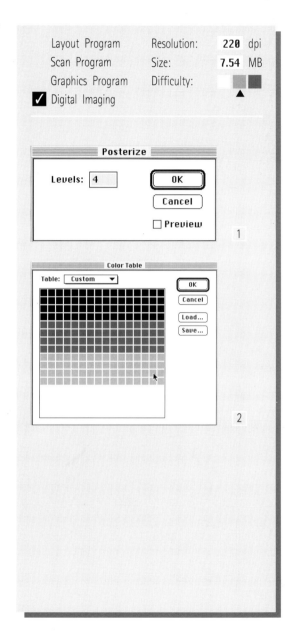

Layout Program
Scan Program
Graphics Program
☑ Digital Imaging

Resolution: **220** dpi
Size: **7.54** MB
Difficulty:

Posterize
Levels: 4   OK
            Cancel
            ☐ Preview
                        1

Color Table
Table: Custom ▼   OK
                   Cancel
                   Load...
                   Save...
                        2

Experimental Posterization

Posterize and add color values to a black-and-white image.

- Open the original halftone in Photoshop. (⌘**O** or **File**)

- Apply the Blur filter. (**Filter>Blur**)

- Select the RGB mode option. (**Mode**)
  Select the Indexed Colors mode option. (**Mode**)

- Open the Posterize dialog box. (**Image>Map**) 1
  Levels: 5

- Open the Color Table dialog box. (**Mode**) 2
  Table: Grayscale
Select a group of squares (values) from a single tonal range.
Choose a first color and a last color from the Color Picker
Click OK. *Photoshop creates a gradient ranging between the
first and last color chosen.*

- Repeat the procedure for all remaining gray levels.

- Open the Posterize dialog box. (**Image>Map**)
  Levels: 8

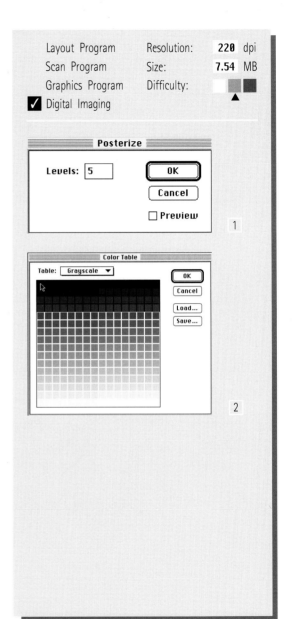

Layout Program	Resolution:	220 dpi
Scan Program	Size:	7.54 MB
Graphics Program	Difficulty:	
✓ Digital Imaging		

LINES AND CONTOURS

Reducing a grayscale image to black-and-white and emphasizing boundary lines is primarily the the job of Photoshop. Programs such as Adobe Illustrator, Adobe Streamline, and FreeHand actually convert the pixel-based Photoshop image into vector-based line art. Of course, how it is done is not so important as what is done with it. The effects generated by either process can produce visually intriguing images.

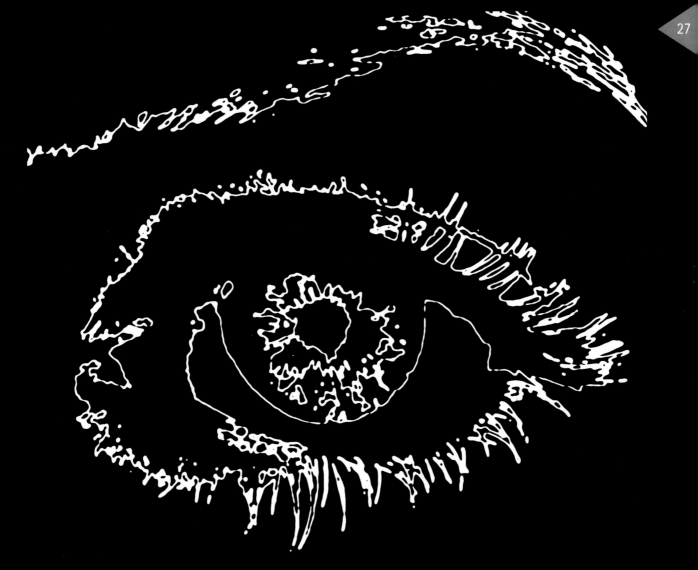

Fine Line Contour Map

- Open the original halftone in Photoshop. (**⌘O** or **File**)

- Apply the Sharpen filter. (**Filter>Sharpen**)
  Repeat. *Shortcut: **⌘F** repeats the last applied filter.*

- Open Levels dialog box. (**⌘L** or **Image>Adjust**) 1
  Input Levels:
  Black: 28   Gamma: 1.00   White: 227

- Apply Trace Contour filter. (**Filter>Stylize**) 2
  Level: 55 *This refers to the tonal value threshold.*
  Edge: Upper *This refers to which side of the threshold to outline.*

▶ *Page 27 (Chapter Title Page): Negative Contours*
*Open the original halftone in Photoshop. (**⌘O** or **File**)*
Set the image threshold:
*Open the Threshold dialog box. (**⌘T** or **Image>Map**) 3*
    Threshold Level: Position slider to desired value.
    See page 16 for further reference.
*Apply the Find Edges filter. (**Filter>Stylize**)*
*Apply the Gaussian Blur filter. (**Filter>Blur**) 4*
    Radius: 3 pixels
*Invert the image. (**⌘I** or **Image>Map**)*

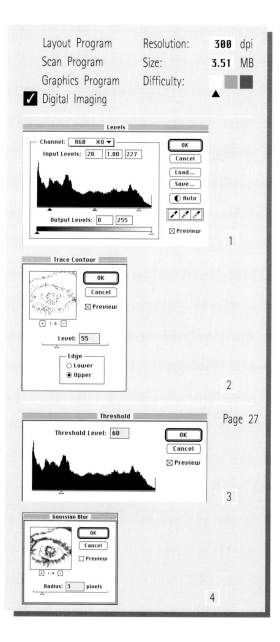

Layout Program	Resolution:	**300** dpi
Scan Program	Size:	**3.51** MB
Graphics Program	Difficulty:	
✓ Digital Imaging		▲

1

2

Page 27

3

4

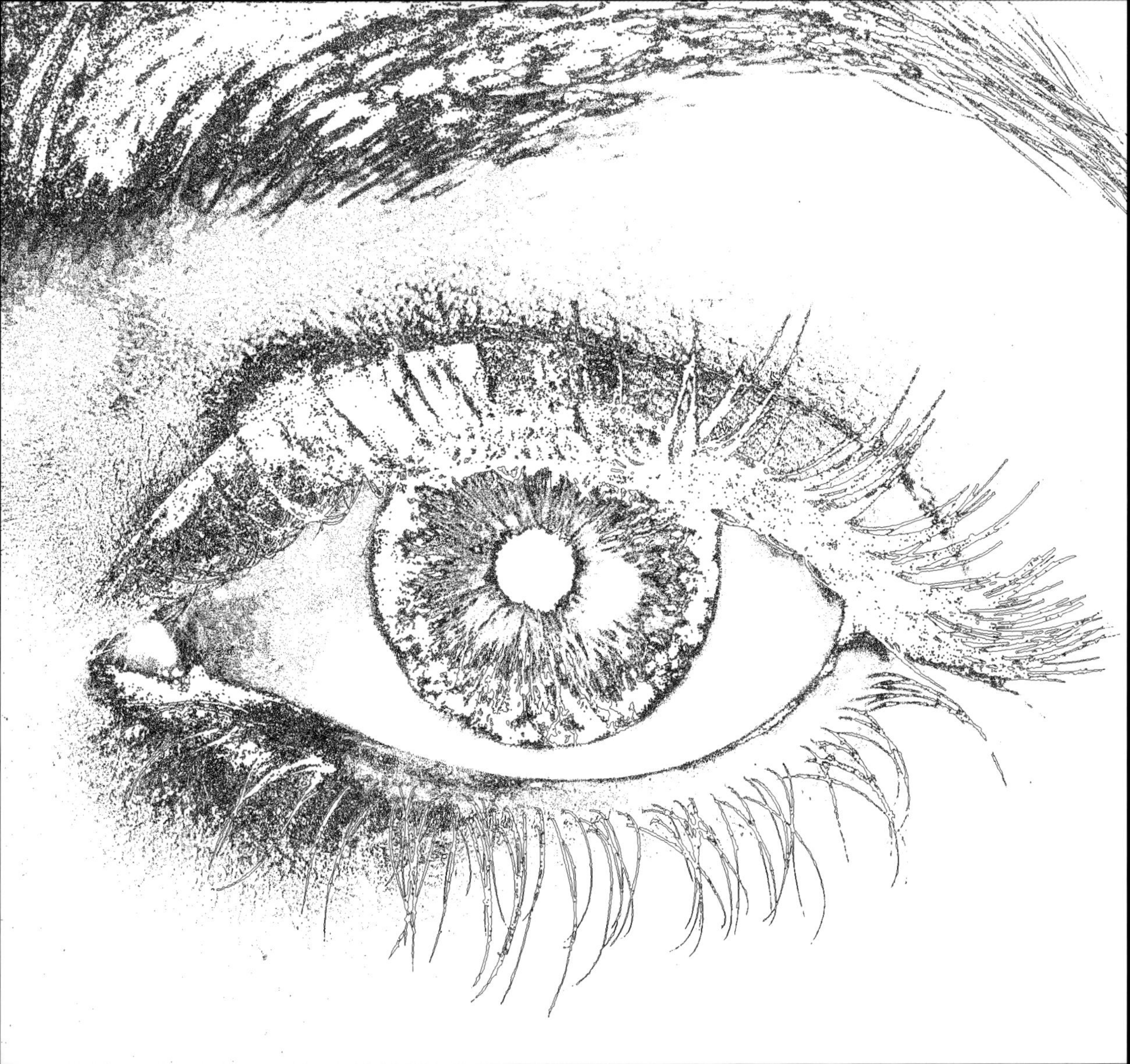

Colored Contours

- Open the original halftone in Photoshop. (⌘O or **File**)
- Select the RGB mode option. (**Mode**)
- Colorize the image:
  Open the Hue/Saturation dialog box. `1`
  (**⌘U** or **Image>Adjust**)
  Select Colorize and use the sliders to adjust the image.
  Hue: 40   Saturation: 100   Lightness: 0

- Apply the Trace Contour filter. (**Filter>Stylize**) `2`
  Level: 55
  Edge: Upper

- Invert the image. (⌘I or **Image>Map**)

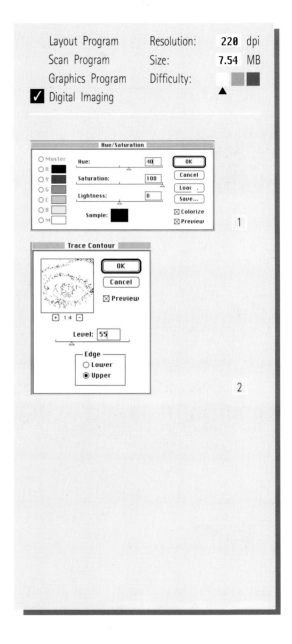

Layout Program	Resolution:	220	dpi
Scan Program	Size:	7.54	MB
Graphics Program	Difficulty:		
✓ Digital Imaging			

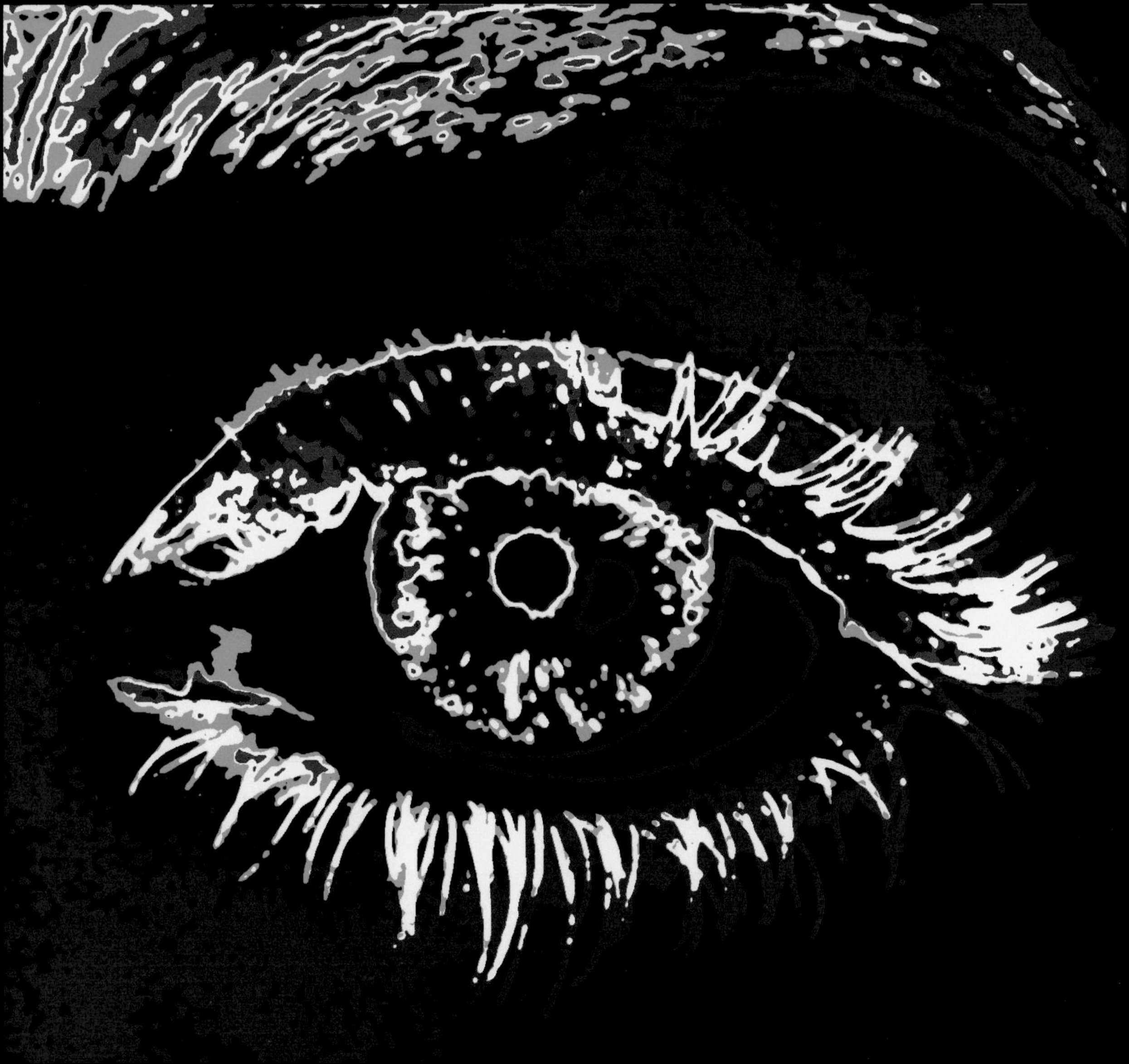

Tracing

- Open the original halftone in FreeHand. (⌘O or **File**)

- Select the image.
  Open the Inspector palette. (⌘I or **Window**) 1
  Choose the Object Inspector.
  Click the Edit button.
  Increase the image contrast.

- Use the Trace tool to select the entire image. 2

- Select and delete the original TIFF image.

- Open the Export dialog box. (⌘E or **Export**) 3
  Name the image "Contours."
  File Format: Adobe Illustrator® 3

- Use "Contours" for the next two examples.

▶*Page 34: Filled Contours*
  Continue with the image from the preceding example.
  Select desired areas. Define a color for the areas:
  Choose a color from the Color Mixer palette. 4
  Drag the swatch to the Color List palette. Then drag the
  color swatch from the Color List to the Fill Selector. 5

▶*Page 35: Line Art/Halftone Combination*
  Open the image "Contours" in Freehand. (⌘O or **File***)*
  Select All of the elements. (⌘A or **Edit***) Group them*
  together. (⌘G or **Arrange***) Define a color for the lines:*
  Choose a color from the Color Mixer palette. 4
  Drag the swatch to the Color List palette. Then drag the
  color swatch from the Color List to the Fill Selector. 5
  Use the Place command to import the original halftone.
  (⌘shift D or **Edit***) Move the original halftone so it*
  covers the tracing. Apply the Send to Back command.
  (⌘B or **Element***)*

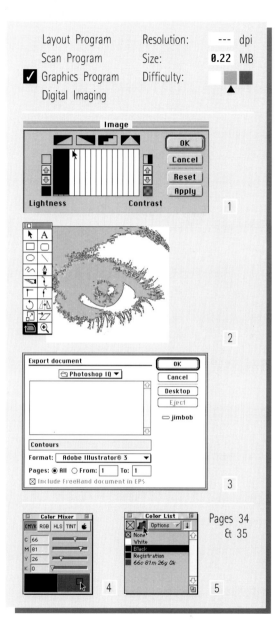

Layout Program
Scan Program
✓ Graphics Program
Digital Imaging

Resolution: --- dpi
Size: 0.22 MB
Difficulty:

1

2

3

Pages 34 & 35

4

5

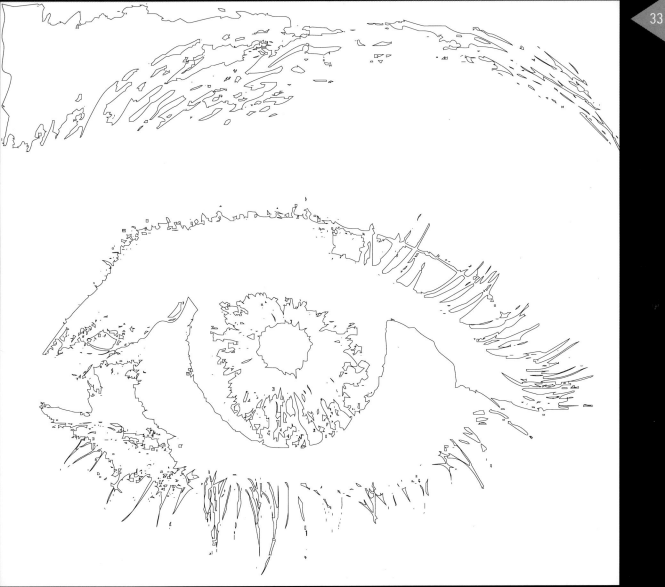

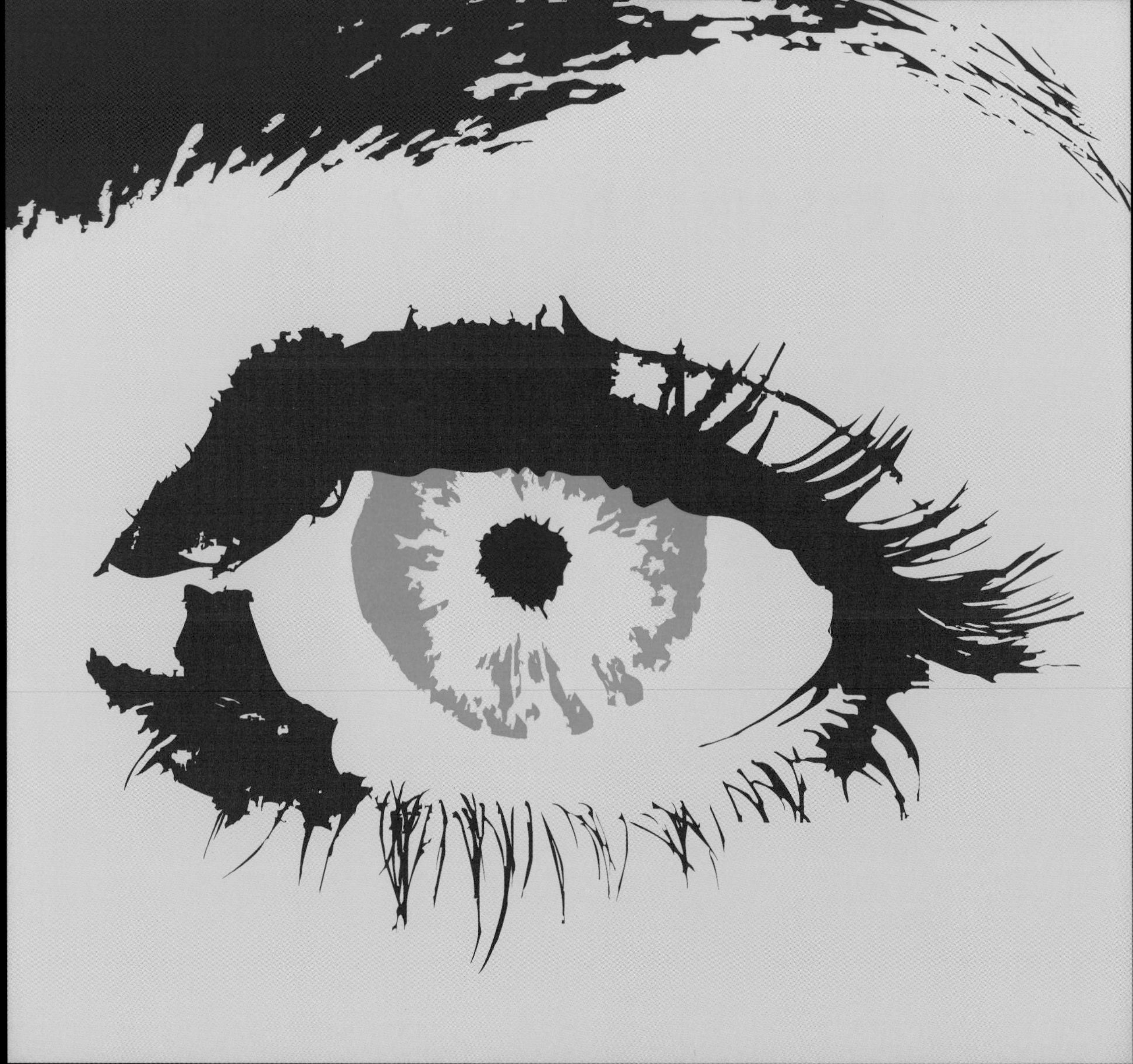

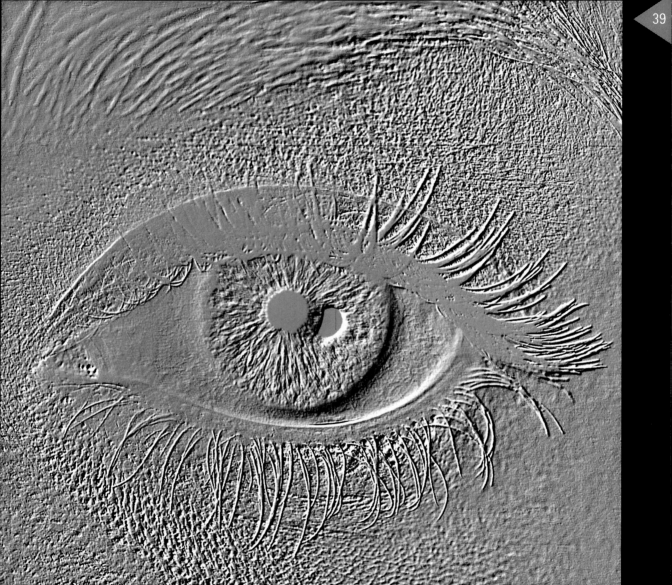

Embossing with Levels

- Open the original halftone in Photoshop. (**⌘O** or **File**)

- Apply the Emboss filter. (**Filter>Stylize**) 1
    Angle: 145°   Height: 4 pixels   Amount: 300%

- Open Levels dialog box. (**⌘L** or **Image>Adjust**) 2
    Input Levels:
    Black: 104   Gamma: 1.00   White: 132

- Open the Posterize dialog box. (**Image>Map**) 3
    Levels: 2

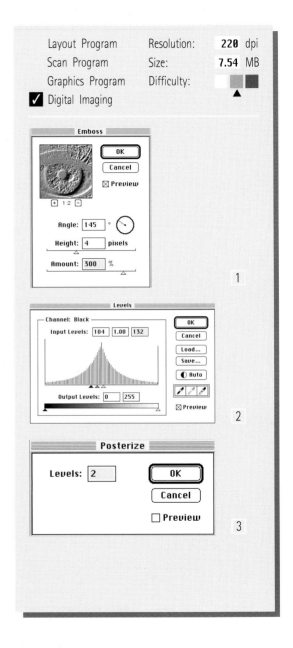

Layout Program	Resolution: **220** dpi
Scan Program	Size: **7.54** MB
Graphics Program	Difficulty:
✔ Digital Imaging	

▶*Page 39 (Chapter Title Page): Halftone Emboss*
*Open the original halftone in Photoshop. (**⌘O** or **File**)*
*Apply the Emboss filter. (**Filter>Stylize**) 1*
    Angle: 145°   Height: 4 pixels   Amount: 300%

Line Embossing

- Open the original halftone in FreeHand as a TIFF. (⌘O or **File**)

- Select all of the image. (⌘A or **Edit**)

- Open the Object Inspector. (⌘I or **Window**)
  Select the Transparent option.
  Click the Edit button.
  Increase the image contrast. 1

- Create a Clone of your image. (⌘= or **Edit**)
  Select the Transparent option from the Object Inspector for the cloned image.

- Change fill color to white:
  Drag the white swatch from the Color List to the Fill Selector or the image. 2

- Offset the white image:
  Select the white image.
  Drag it up and to the left.

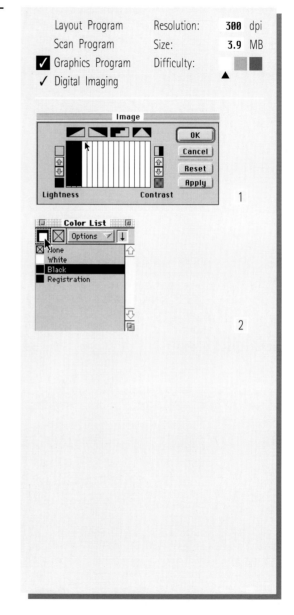

Layout Program	Resolution:	300	dpi
Scan Program	Size:	3.9	MB
✓ Graphics Program	Difficulty:		
✓ Digital Imaging			

Metal Stamp

- Open the original halftone in Photoshop. (⌘**O** or **File**)

- Apply the Gaussian Blur filter. (**Filter>Blur**) 1
    Radius: 10 pixels

- Apply the Find Edges filter. (**Filter>Stylize**)

- Open the Levels dialog box. (⌘**L** or **Image>Adjust**) 2
    Input Levels:
    Black: 190   Gamma: 1.00   White: 255

- Invert the image. (⌘**I** or **Image>Map**)

- Open the Brightness/Contrast dialog box.
    (⌘**B** or **Image>Adjust**) 3
    Brightness: 0   Contrast: 100

- Apply the Emboss filter. (**Filter>Stylize**) 4
    Angle: -40°   Height: 10 pixels   Amount: 100%

- Select the CMYK mode option. (**Mode**)
    Open the Hue/Saturation dialog box.
    (⌘**U** or **Image>Adjust**) 5
    Select Colorize and use the sliders to adjust the image.

- Open the Channels palette. (**Window>Palettes**)
    Create a new Channel. Name it "Mask."

- Select the Lasso tool. Hold the option key and select a
    diagonal area across the image. Use the Gradient tool to fill
    the selected area. Repeat over the entire image.

- Select None. (⌘**D** or **Select**)

- Target the CMYK channel on the Channels palette.
    Execute the Load Selection. (**Select**)
    Inverse the selection. (**Select**)

- Open Levels dialog box. (⌘**L** or **Image>Adjust**)
    Input Levels: Black: 0   Gamma: 0.70   White: 255

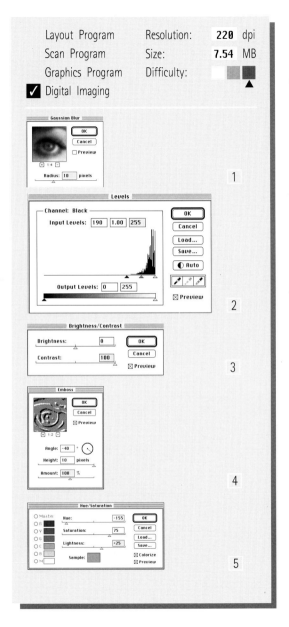

Layout Program   Resolution: 220 dpi
Scan Program   Size: 7.54 MB
Graphics Program   Difficulty:
✓ Digital Imaging

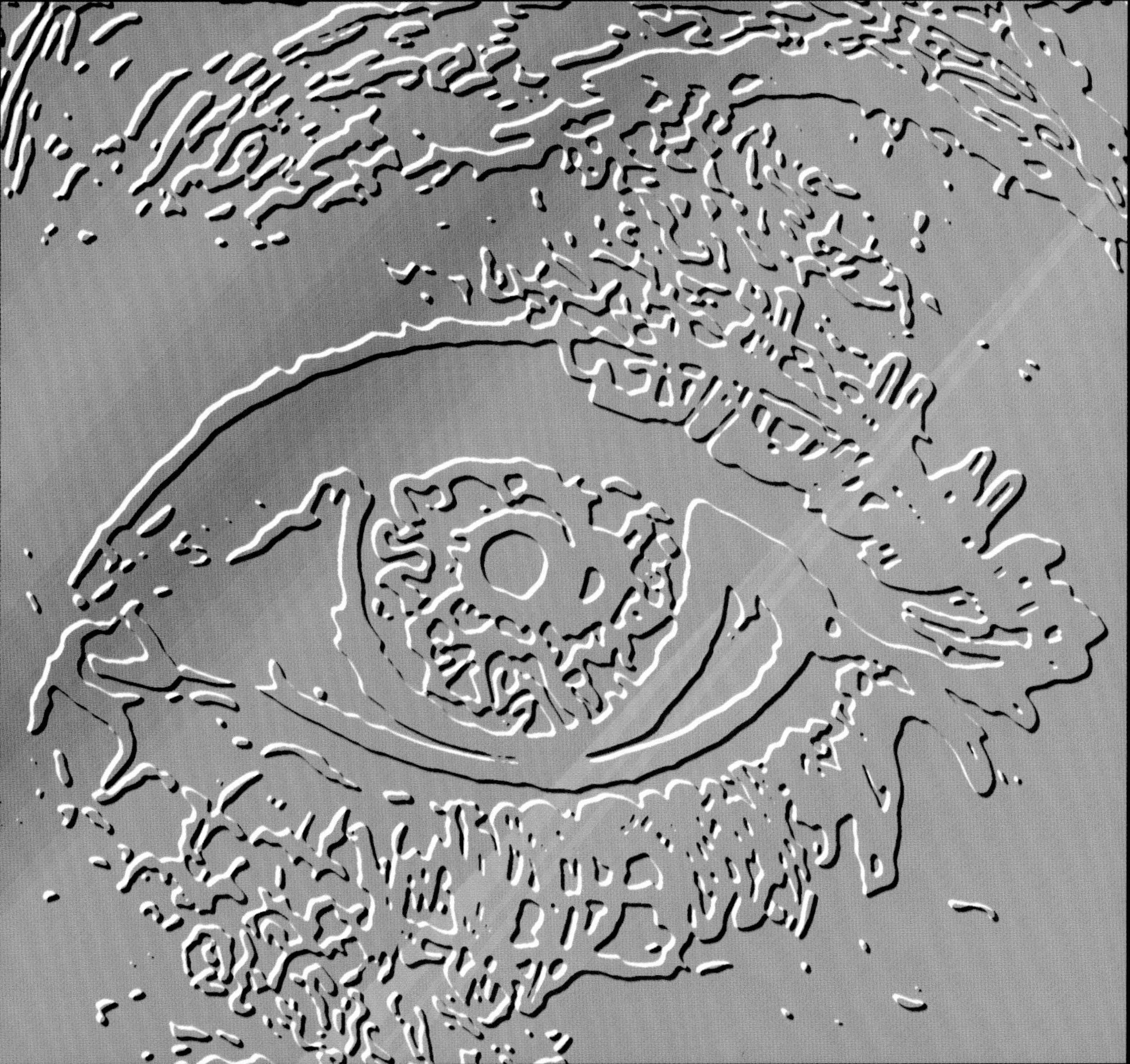

Metal Embossing

- Open the original halftone in Photoshop. (**⌘O** or **File**)

- Apply the Gaussian Blur filter. (**Filter>Blur**) 1
    Radius: 10 pixels

- Apply the Find Edges filter. (**Filter>Stylize**)

- Open the Levels dialog box. (**⌘L** or **Image>Adjust**) 2
    Input Levels:
    Black: 190   Gamma: 1.00   White: 255

- Open the Curves dialog box. (**⌘M** or **Image>Adjust**) 3
    Click on the curve, add points, and adjust the
    dynamic of the curve.

- Select the CMYK mode option. (**Mode**)

- Open the Hue/Saturation dialog box.
    (**⌘U** or **Image>Adjust**) 4
    Select Colorize and use the sliders to adjust the image.

- Open the Levels dialog box. (**⌘L** or **Image>Adjust**)
    Increase black Input Levels and decrease white Input Levels
    by moving sliders toward the middle.

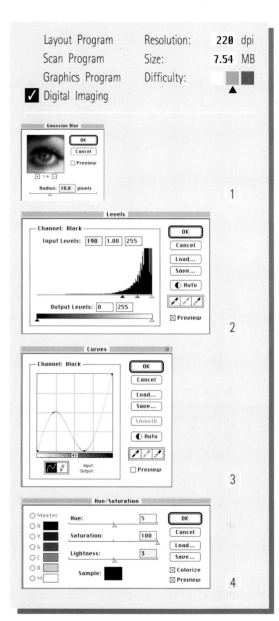

Layout Program	Resolution:	220	dpi
Scan Program	Size:	7.54	MB
Graphics Program	Difficulty:		
✓ Digital Imaging			

Marble Embossing

- Scan a black and white picture of a marble texture.
  Make the file the same size and resolution as the original
  halftone. Open the scan in Photoshop. (**⌘O** or **File**) 1

- Open the original halftone in Photoshop. (**⌘O** or **File**)
  Open the Brightness/Contrast dialog box. 2
  (**⌘B** or **Image>Adjust**) Brightness: 50   Contrast: 100

- Select All (**⌘A** or **Select**) and Copy (**⌘C** or **Edit**) the image.
  Open the Channels palette. (**Window>Palettes**)
  Create three new channels.
  Name them "Eye Line Art," "Light Edge," and "Shadow Edge."
  Paste the copied image into each channel. (**⌘V** or **Edit**)

- Target the channel "Light Edge." 3
  Apply the Emboss filter. (**Filter>Stylize**)
          Angle: -45°   Height: 7 pixels   Amount: 100%
  Open the Levels dialog box. (**⌘L** or **Image>Adjust**) 4
          Input Levels: Black: 253   Gamma: 1.00   White: 255

- Target the channel "Shadow Edge." Repeat the Emboss filter.
  Shortcut: **⌘F** *repeats the last performed filter.*
  Open the Levels dialog box. (**⌘L** or **Image>Adjust**) 5
          Input Levels: Black: 0   Gamma: 1.00   White: 2

- Target the marble image.
  Select All (**⌘A** or **Select**) and Copy (**⌘C** or **Edit**) the image.
  Target the original image. Target the Black Channel.
  Paste the copied image into the channel. (**⌘V** or **Edit**)

- Load Selection "Eye Line Art" channel. (**Select**)
  Shortcut: Hold the option key and click on the channel.
  Inverse the selection. (**Select**)
  Open the Levels dialog box. (**⌘L** or **Image>Adjust**)
          Input Levels: Black: 80   Gamma: 1.00   White: 255

- Load Selection "Light Edge" channel. (**Select**)
  Open the Levels dialog box. (**⌘L** or **Image>Adjust**)
          Input Levels: Black: 0   Gamma: 1.00   White: 80

- Load Selection "Shadow Edge" channel. (**Select**)
  Inverse the selection. (**Select**)
  Open the Levels dialog box. (**⌘L** or **Image>Adjust**)
          Input Levels: Black: 100   Gamma: 1.00   White: 255

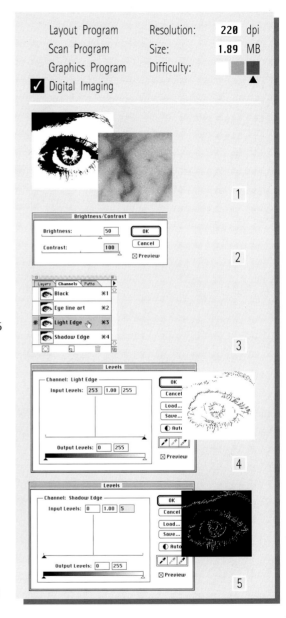

Layout Program	Resolution: **220** dpi
Scan Program	Size: **1.89** MB
Graphics Program	Difficulty:
✓ Digital Imaging	▲

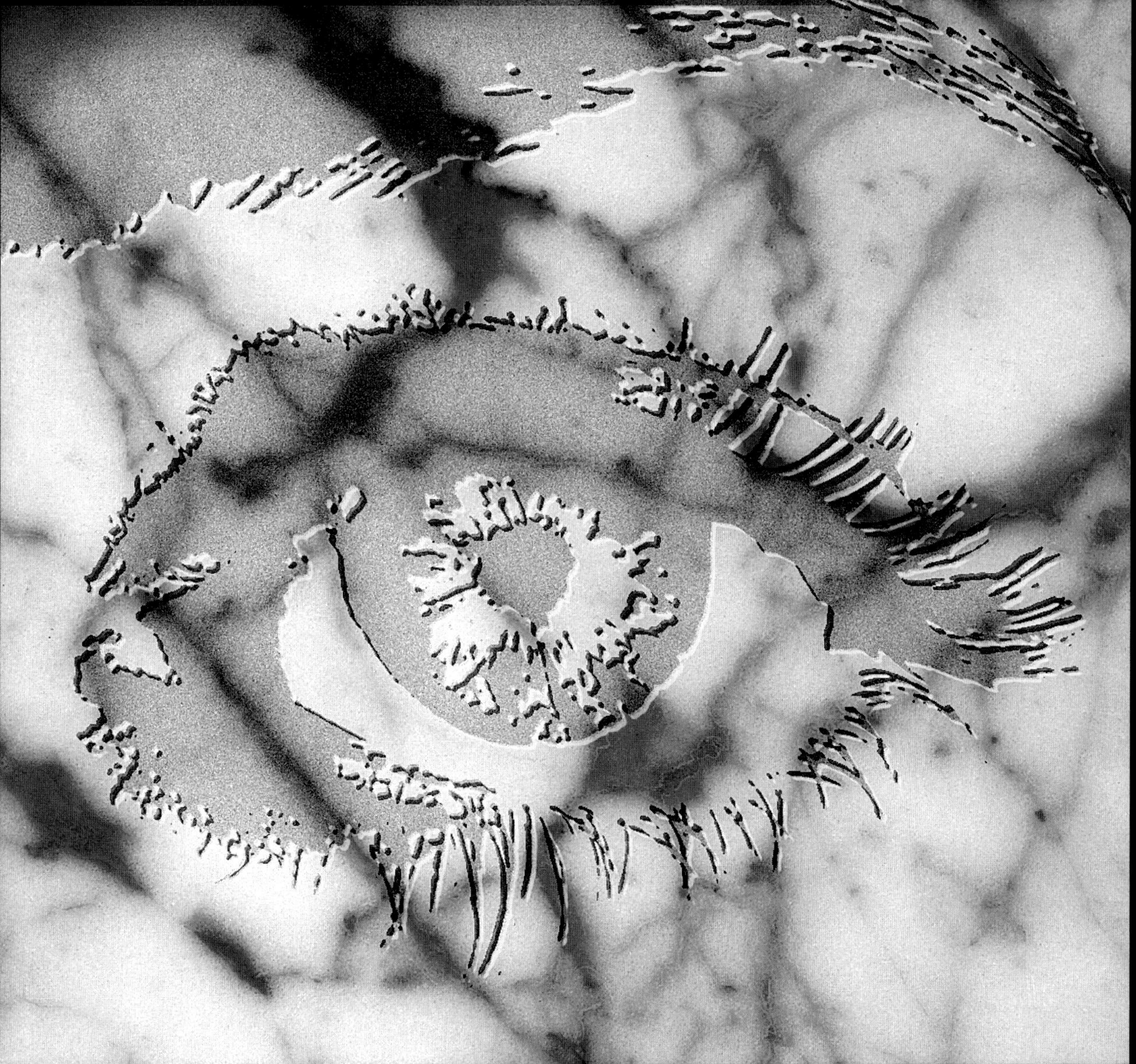

Screening

When an image is screened, all gray levels are converted into lines, dots, or squares of varying densities and sizes. This kind of screening is used to prepare halftone images for printing. Using extreme enlargements and combining the various screen shapes can create a wide variety of graphic effects.

Basic Screen

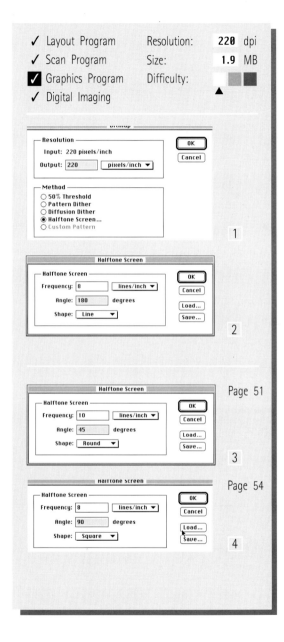

✓ Layout Program   Resolution: **220** dpi
✓ Scan Program   Size: **1.9** MB
☑ Graphics Program   Difficulty:
✓ Digital Imaging

- Open the original halftone in Photoshop. (⌘**O** or **File**)

- Select the Bitmap mode option. (**Mode**)   1
    Output: 220 pixels/inch
    Method: Halftone Screen
  Click OK. *This opens the halftone dialog box.*   2
    Frequency: 8   Angle: 180°   Shape: Line

▶ *Page 51 (Chapter Title Page): Coarse Dot Screen*
  *Open the original halftone in Photoshop. (⌘**O** or **File**)*
  *Select the Bitmap mode option. (**Mode**) 1*
    Output: 220 pixels/inch
    Method: Halftone Screen
  Click OK. This opens the halftone dialog box. 3
    Frequency: 10   Angle: 45°   Shape: Round

▶ *Page 54: Square Screen*
  *Open the original halftone in Photoshop. (⌘**O** or **File**)*
  *Select the Bitmap mode option. (**Mode**) 1*
    Output: 220 pixels/inch
    Method: Halftone Screen
  Click OK. This opens the halftone dialog box. 4
    Frequency: 8   Angle: 90°   Shape: Square

53

Matrix Screen

- Open the original halftone in Photoshop. (⌘O or **File**)

- Select the Bitmap mode option. (**Mode**) 1
	Output: 40 pixels/inch
	Method: Pattern Dither
This produces a bitmapped image that converts the grayscale tonal values into geometric arrangements of black-and-white dots.

▶ *Page 55: Line Screen-Line Art Combination*
*Open the original halftone in Photoshop. (⌘O or **File**)*
*Select All (⌘A or **Select**) and Copy (⌘C or **Edit**) the image.*
*Select the Bitmap mode option. (**Mode**) 2*
	Output: 220 pixels/inch Method: Halftone Screen
Click OK. This opens the halftone dialog box. 3
	Frequency: 8 Angle: 45° Shape: Line
*Select the Grayscale mode option. (**Mode**)*
*Open the Channels palette. (**Window> Palettes**)*
Create a new Channel.
*Paste the copied image into the new Channel. (⌘V or **Edit**)*
Open the Brightness/Contrast dialog box.
(⌘B *or* **Image>Adjust)**
	Brightness: 50 Contrast: 100
*Invert the image. (⌘I or **Image>Map**)*
Select the Channels palette. Target the Black Channel.   4
Select the Layers palette. Target the Background Layer.
*Load Selection to the layer. (**Select**) Delete the Selection.*
*Select the CMYK mode option. (**Mode**)*
Click on the Foreground color swatch and choose a color. 5
*Apply a Fill. (**Edit**) 6*
Shortcut: Shift & Delete brings up the Fill dialog box.
	Use: Foreground Color Opacity: 100%
	Paint mode:Normal

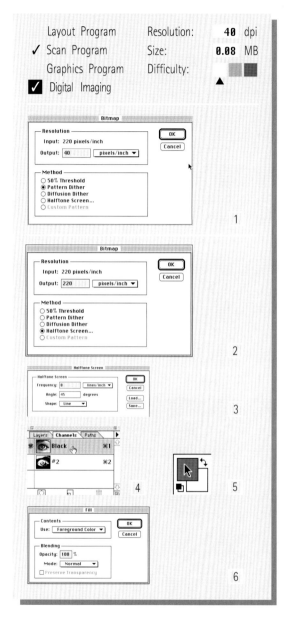

Layout Program   Resolution: **40** dpi
✓ Scan Program   Size: **0.08** MB
Graphics Program   Difficulty:
✓ Digital Imaging   ▲

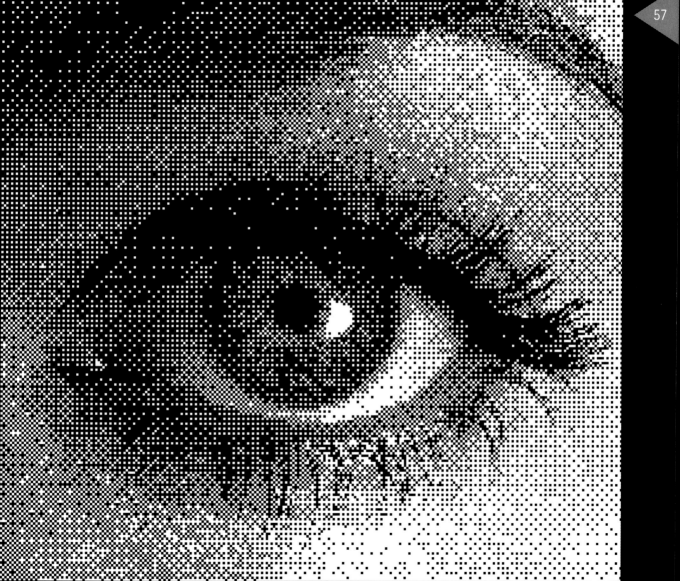

Grain Screen

- Open the original halftone in Photoshop. (**⌘O** or **File**)

- Apply the High Pass filter. (**Filter>Other**) 1
  Radius: 10 pixels

- Open the Levels dialog box. (**⌘L** or **Image>Adjust**) 2
  Input Levels:
  Black: 118   Gamma: 0.97   White: 179

- Select the Bitmap mode option. (**Mode**)
  Output: 50 pixels/inch   Method: Diffusion Dither

- Select the Grayscale mode option. (**Mode**)

- Set the Image Size. (**Image**) 3
  Constrain: Proportions
  Resolution: 600 pixels/inch

- Open the Levels dialog box. (**⌘L** or **Image>Adjust**) 4
  Input Levels: Black: Move gradually to the right.
  Gamma: 1.00   White: 255

- Select the Bitmap mode option. (**Mode**)
  Output: 600 pixels/inch   Method: 50% Threshold

▶ *Page 60: Grain Screen*
  *Open the original halftone in Photoshop. (**⌘O** or **File**)*
  *Select the Bitmap mode option. (**Mode**)*
      Output: 100 pixels/inch   Method: Diffusion Dither

▶ *Page 61: Grain Screen with Contour Lines*
  *Open the original halftone in Photoshop. (**⌘O** or **File**)*
  *Select the Lab Color mode option. (**Mode**)*
  The conversion will provide three image channels:
  L (lightness), a (green to red), and b (blue).
  *Apply the Find Edges filter. (**Filter>Stylize**)*
  *Select the Grayscale mode option. (**Mode**)*
  *Select the Bitmap mode option. (**Mode**)*
      Output: 100 pixels/inch   Method: Diffusion Dither

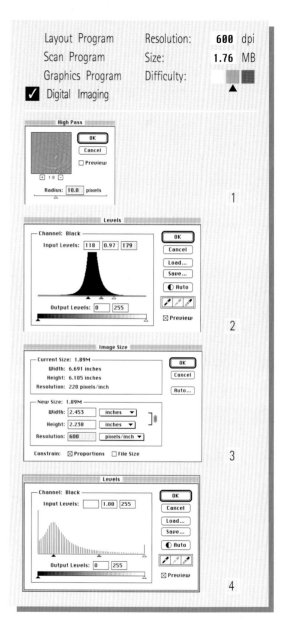

Layout Program	Resolution:	**600**	dpi
Scan Program	Size:	**1.76**	MB
Graphics Program	Difficulty:		
☑ Digital Imaging			

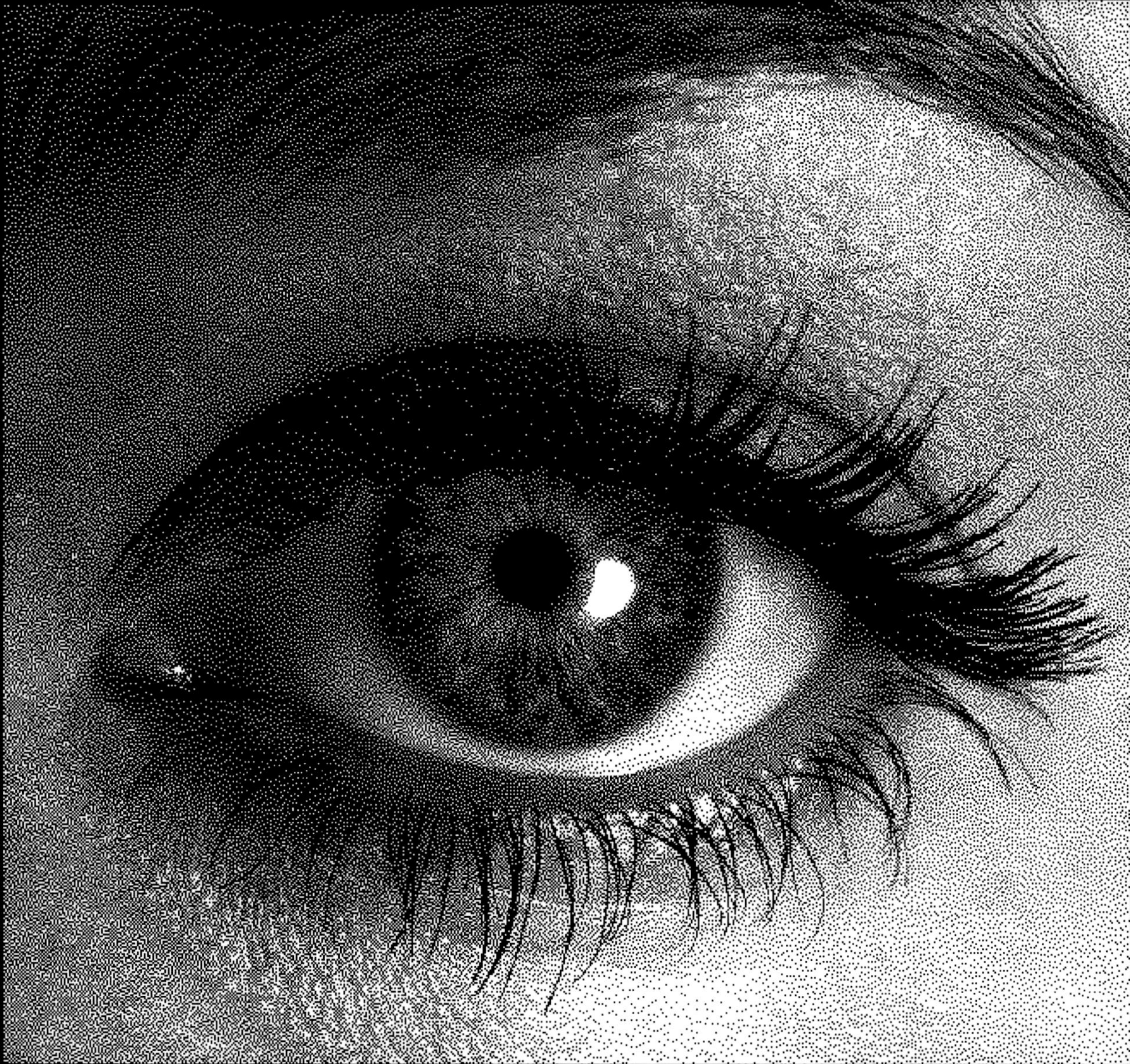

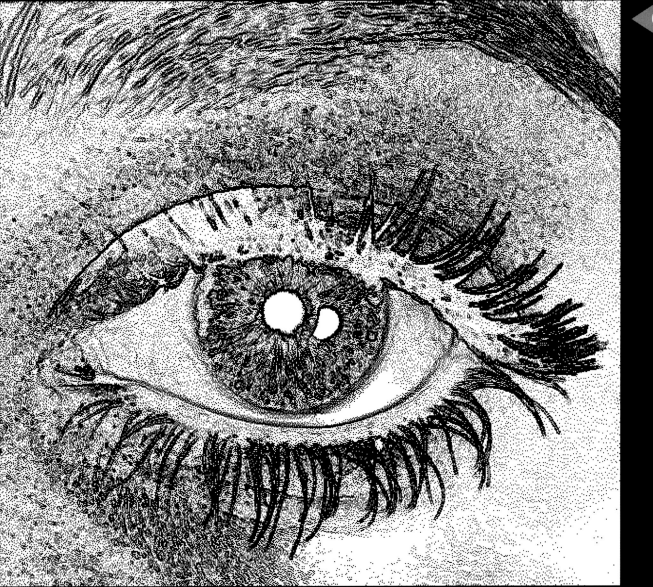

Random Screen

Layout Program   Resolution: **600** dpi
Scan Program   Size: **1.75** MB
Graphics Program   Difficulty:
☑ Digital Imaging

- Open the original halftone in Photoshop. (⌘**O** or **File**)

- Select the Bitmap mode option. (**Mode**) 1
    Output: 25 pixels/inch
    Method: Diffusion Dither
    This converts the grayscale tonal values into a random
    grainy texture of black-and-white dots.

- Select the Grayscale mode option. (**Mode**)

- Choose the Image Size. (**Image**) 2
    Constrain: Proportions
    Resolution: 600 pixels/inch

- Open the Levels dialog box. (⌘**L** or **Image>Adjust**) 3
    Input Levels:
    Black: 65   Gamma: 1.00   White: 92

- Select the Bitmap mode option. (**Mode**)
    Output: 600 pixels/inch
    Method: 50% Threshold

A similar effect can also be achieved with a hands-on
approach: Print a reduced randomized version of the image
on an ink-jet printer. Then enlarge it again on a photocopier
or scanner.

Bitmap

Resolution
Input: 220 pixels/inch
Output: 25   pixels/inch
OK
Cancel

Method
○ 50% Threshold
○ Pattern Dither
● Diffusion Dither
○ Halftone Screen...
○ Custom Pattern

1

Image Size

Current Size: 25K
Width: 6.68 inches
Height: 6.12 inches
Resolution: 25 pixels/inch
OK
Cancel
Auto...

New Size: 25K
Width: 0.278 inches
Height: 0.255 inches
Resolution: 600 pixels/inch

Constrain: ☒ Proportions ☐ File Size

2

Levels

Channel: Black
Input Levels: 65 1.00 92
OK
Cancel
Load...
Save...
Auto

Output Levels: 0 255
☒ Preview

3

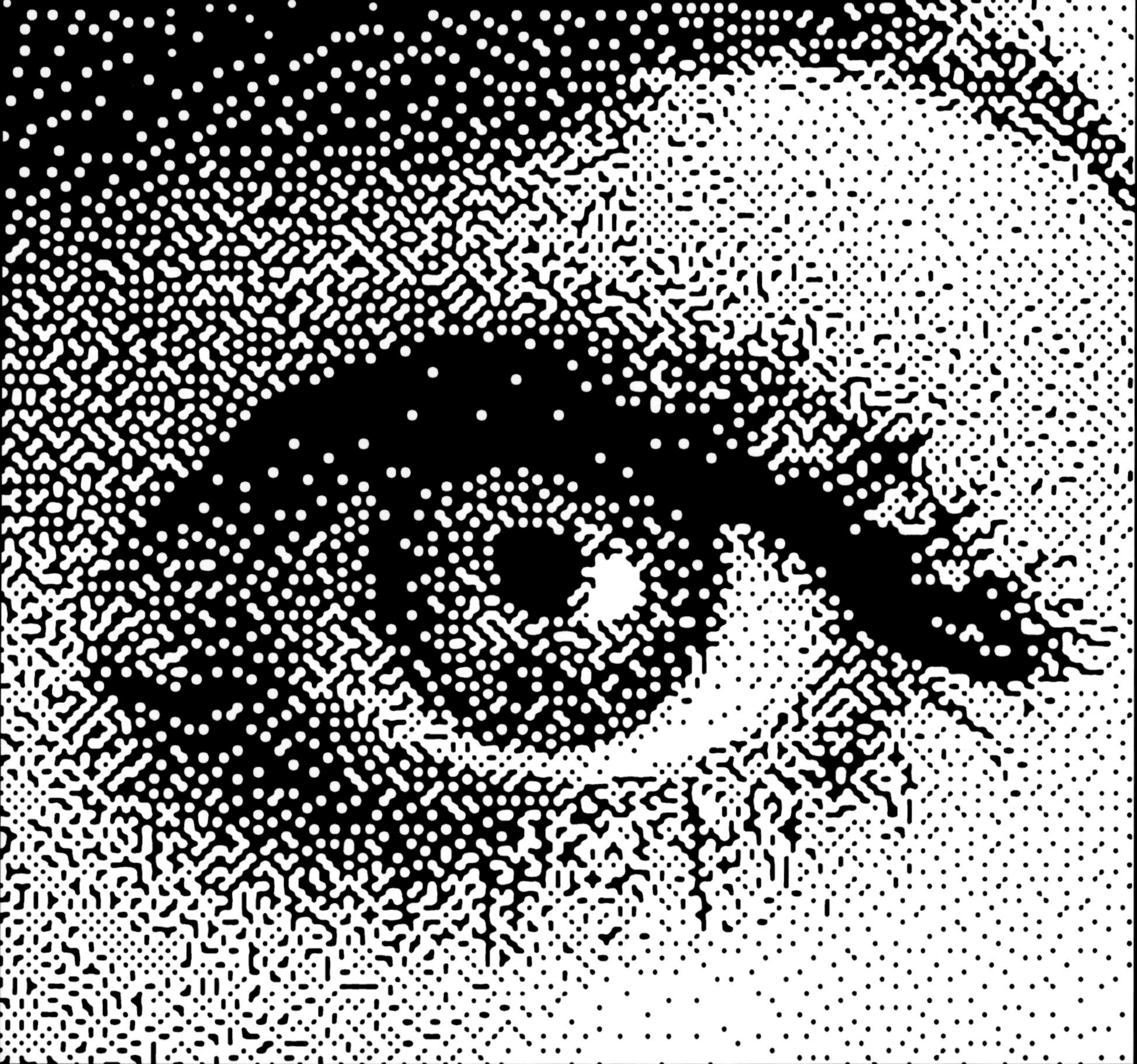

Mosaic Effects

- Open the original halftone in Photoshop. (⌘O or **File**)

- Open the Levels dialog box. (⌘L or **Image>Adjust**) 1
  Increase the black Input Levels, decrease white Input Levels.

- Reduce the image resolution:
  Choose Image Size. (**Image**) 2
       Constrain: Proportions
       Resolution: 10 pixels/inch

- Apply the Sharpen More filter. (**Filter>Sharpen**)

- Use your results for the examples on pages 66 & 67.

▶ *Page 66: 2-bit Mosaic*
Proceed with the resulting image from "Mosaic Effects."
Open the Brightness/Contrast dialog box.
(⌘B *or* **Image>Adjust)** 3
    Brightness: 0
    Contrast: 100

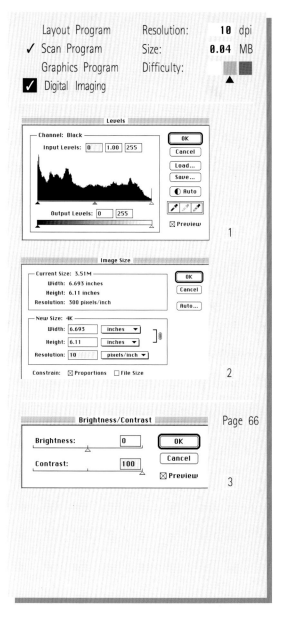

Layout Program   Resolution: **10** dpi
✓ Scan Program   Size: **0.04** MB
Graphics Program   Difficulty:
✓ Digital Imaging

Levels
Channel: Black
Input Levels: 0   1.00   255
OK / Cancel / Load... / Save... / ◐ Auto
Output Levels: 0   255
⊠ Preview
1

Image Size
Current Size: 3.51M
Width: 6.693 inches
Height: 6.11 inches
Resolution: 300 pixels/inch
OK / Cancel / Auto...
New Size: 4K
Width: 6.693   inches
Height: 6.11   inches
Resolution: 10   pixels/inch
Constrain: ⊠ Proportions ☐ File Size
2

Page 66

Brightness/Contrast
Brightness: 0
Contrast: 100
OK / Cancel / ⊠ Preview
3

Pointillist

- Open the original halftone in Photoshop. (**⌘O** or **File**)

- Select the CMYK mode option. (**Mode**)

- Apply the Pointillize filter. (**Filter>Pixelate**) 1
    Cell Size: 17

- Apply the Crystallize filter. (**Filter>Pixelate**) 2
    Cell Size: 17

Page 67: Detail Mosaic
Proceed with the resulting image from "Mosaic Effects"on pages 64-65.
*Reduce the image resolution: Choose Image Size. (**Image**)*
    Constrain: Proportions   Resolution: 72 pixels/inch
*Apply the Unsharp Mask filter. (**Filter>Sharpen**) 3*
    Amount: 50%   Radius: 1 pixel   Threshold: 0 levels
Apply this filter a total of four times.
Shortcut: Use ⌘F to reapply your last used filter.
Apply the following filters in this order:
*Add Noise filter (**Filter>Noise**) 4*
    Amount: 32   Distribution: Gaussian
*Maximum Filter (**Filter>Other**)*
    Radius: 1 pixel
*Minimum filter (**Filter>Other**)*
    Radius: 1 pixel
*Unsharp Mask filter. (**Filter>Sharpen**)*
    Amount: 50%   Radiùs: 1 pixel   Threshold: 0 levels
*Select the RGB mode option. (**Mode**)*
*Select the Indexed Colors mode option. (**Mode**) 5*
*Open the Hue/Saturation dialog box. (**⌘U** or **Image>Adjust**)*
Select Colorize and use the sliders to adjust the image.

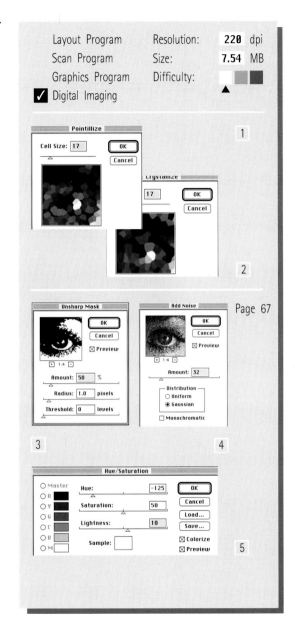

Layout Program	Resolution: **220** dpi
Scan Program	Size: **7.54** MB
Graphics Program	Difficulty:
✓ Digital Imaging	

Page 67

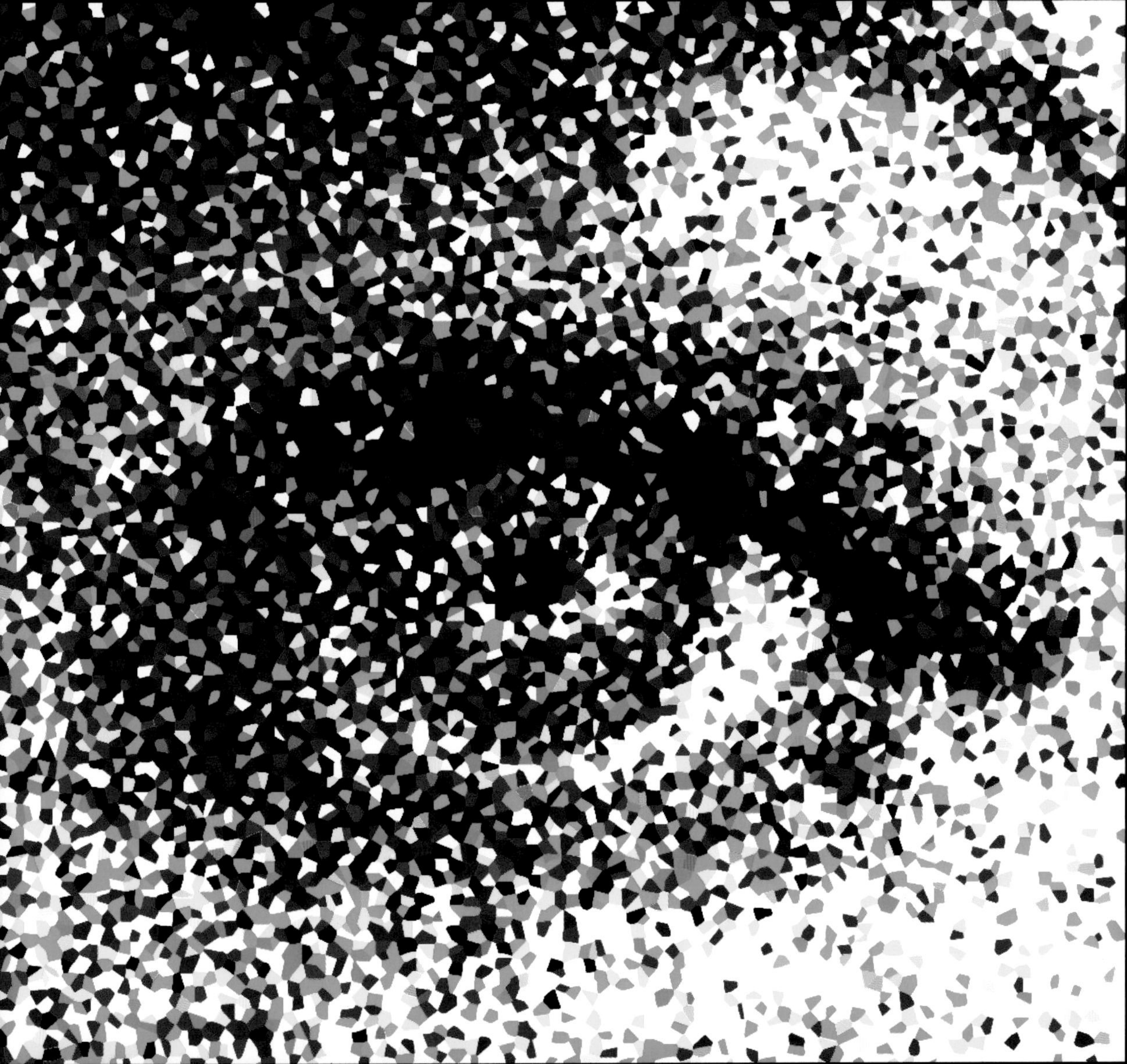

Color Halftone Gradient

- Open the original halftone in Photoshop. (⌘O or **File**)

- Use the Lasso tool to select a triangular area in the upper right half of the image. *Hold the Option key and click on three appropriate points.*

- Apply a Feather to the selection. (**Select**) 1
    Radius: 100 pixels

- Select the CMYK mode option. (**Mode**)

- Apply the Color Halftone filter. (**Filter>Pixelate**) 2
    Max Radius: 25 pixels
    Use default screen angles.

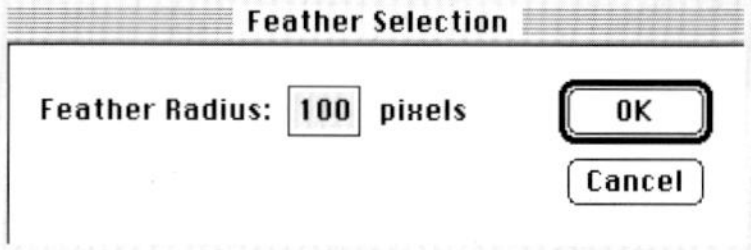

Layout Program	Resolution:	**220**	dpi
Scan Program	Size:	**7.54**	MB
Graphics Program	Difficulty:		
✓ Digital Imaging			

Feather Selection

Feather Radius: [100] pixels   [OK]
[Cancel]   1

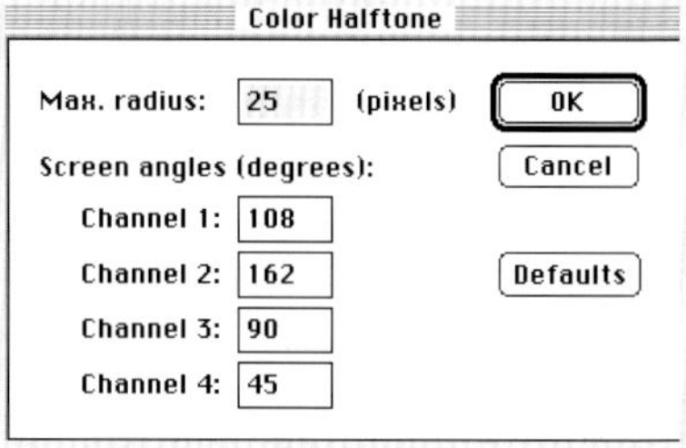

Color Halftone

Max. radius: [25] (pixels)   [OK]
Screen angles (degrees):   [Cancel]
    Channel 1: [108]
    Channel 2: [162]   [Defaults]
    Channel 3: [90]
    Channel 4: [45]
                                             2

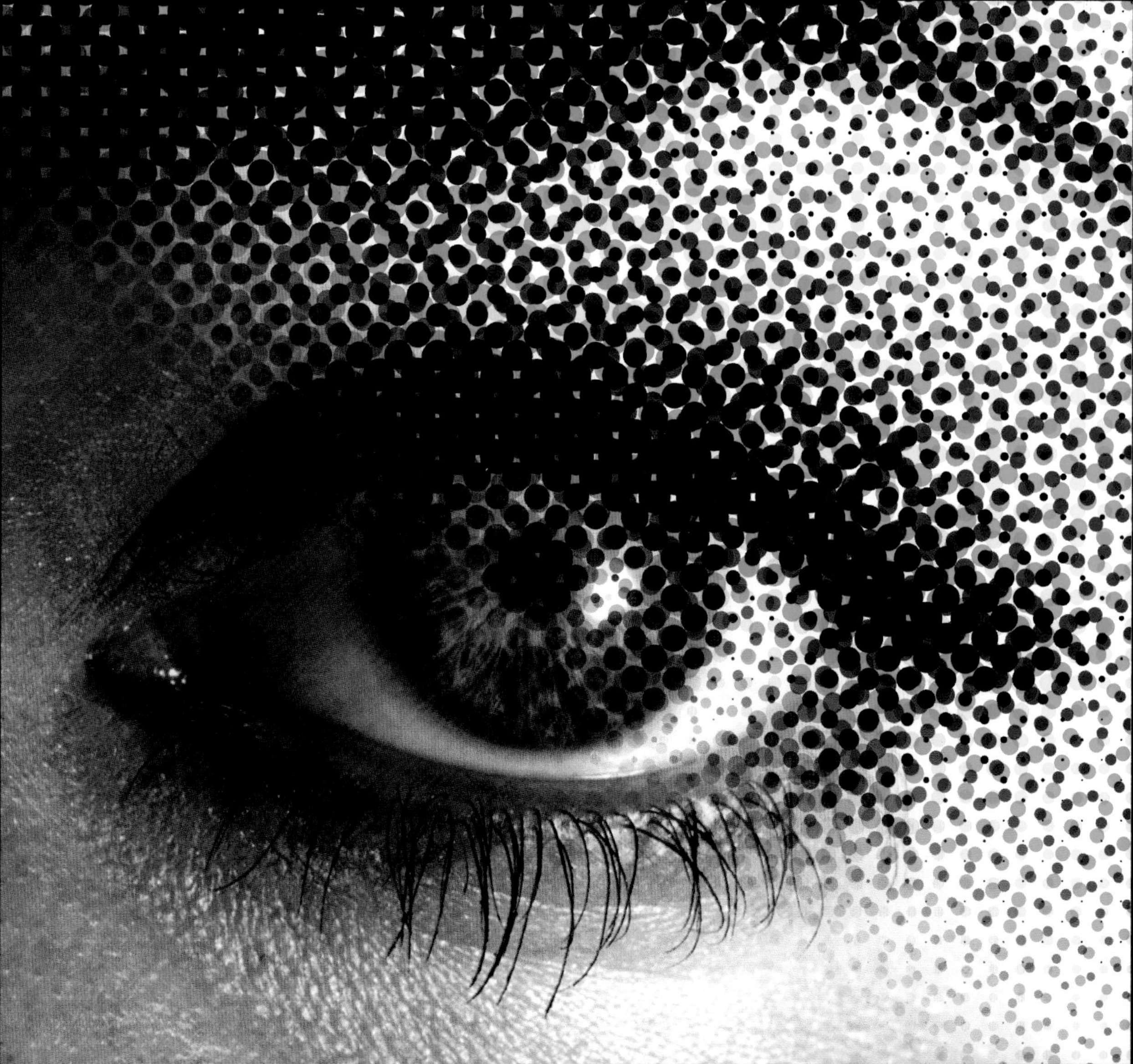

Shifted Pointillization

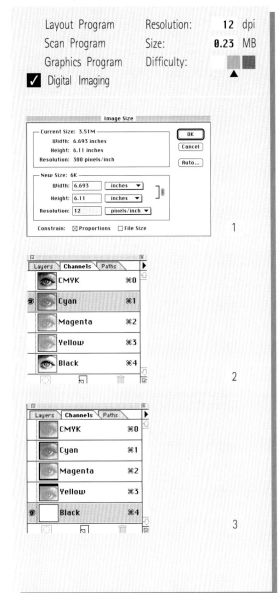

Layout Program   Resolution: **12** dpi
Scan Program   Size: **0.23** MB
Graphics Program   Difficulty:
☑ Digital Imaging

- Open the original halftone in Photoshop. (⌘**O** or **File**)

- Reduce the image resolution:
  Choose Image Size. (**Image**) 1
      Constrain: Proportions
      Resolution: 12 pixels/inch

- Select the CMYK mode option. (**Mode**)

- Target the Cyan Channel. 2
  Offset the channel using the Move tool or by applying the
  Offset filter. (**Filter>Other**)

- Target the Yellow and Magenta channels and offset each in
  a different direction.

- Target the Black Channel. 3
  Select All (⌘**A** or **Select**)
  Delete the selection.

- Target the CMYK channel.
  Select Auto Levels. (**Image>Adjust**)

SCREEN STRUCTURES

Similar results to those described in the Screening chapter can be achieved without converting the gray levels into lines or dots. Combining scanned images or line art with halftones can produce interesting enhancements to images.

Pen and Ink

Layout Program
Scan Program
Graphics Program
☑ Digital Imaging

Resolution: **300** dpi
Size: **0.45** MB
Difficulty:

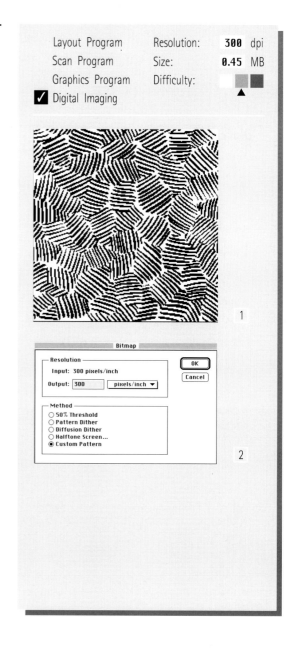

1

- Scan a pen and ink pattern in black and white. 1
  Make sure this file is the same size and resolution as the original halftone.

- Open the scan in Photoshop. (⌘**O** or **File**)

- Select the Grayscale mode option. (**Mode**)

- Apply the Blur More filter. (**Filter>Blur**)

- Further distort the pattern by increasing the contrast.
  Open the Levels dialog box. (⌘**L** or **Image>Adjust**)
  Increase the black Input Levels and decrease white Input Levels by sliding them toward the middle.
  Click OK. *The image contrast will increase.*

- Define this image as a fill pattern:
  Select the entire pen and ink pattern. (⌘**A** or **Select**)
  Apply Define Pattern. (**Edit**)

- Open the original halftone in Photoshop. (⌘**O** or **File**)

- Select the Bitmap mode option. (**Mode**) 2
    Output: 300 pixels/inch
    Method: Custom Pattern

Bitmap

Resolution
  Input: 300 pixels/inch
  Output: 300   pixels/inch ▾

OK
Cancel

Method
  ○ 50% Threshold
  ○ Pattern Dither
  ○ Diffusion Dither
  ○ Halftone Screen...
  ● Custom Pattern

2

▶ *Page 75 (Chapter Title Page): Wood Grain*
  Scan a wood grain texture in place of the pen and ink sketch pattern.
  Proceed as above.

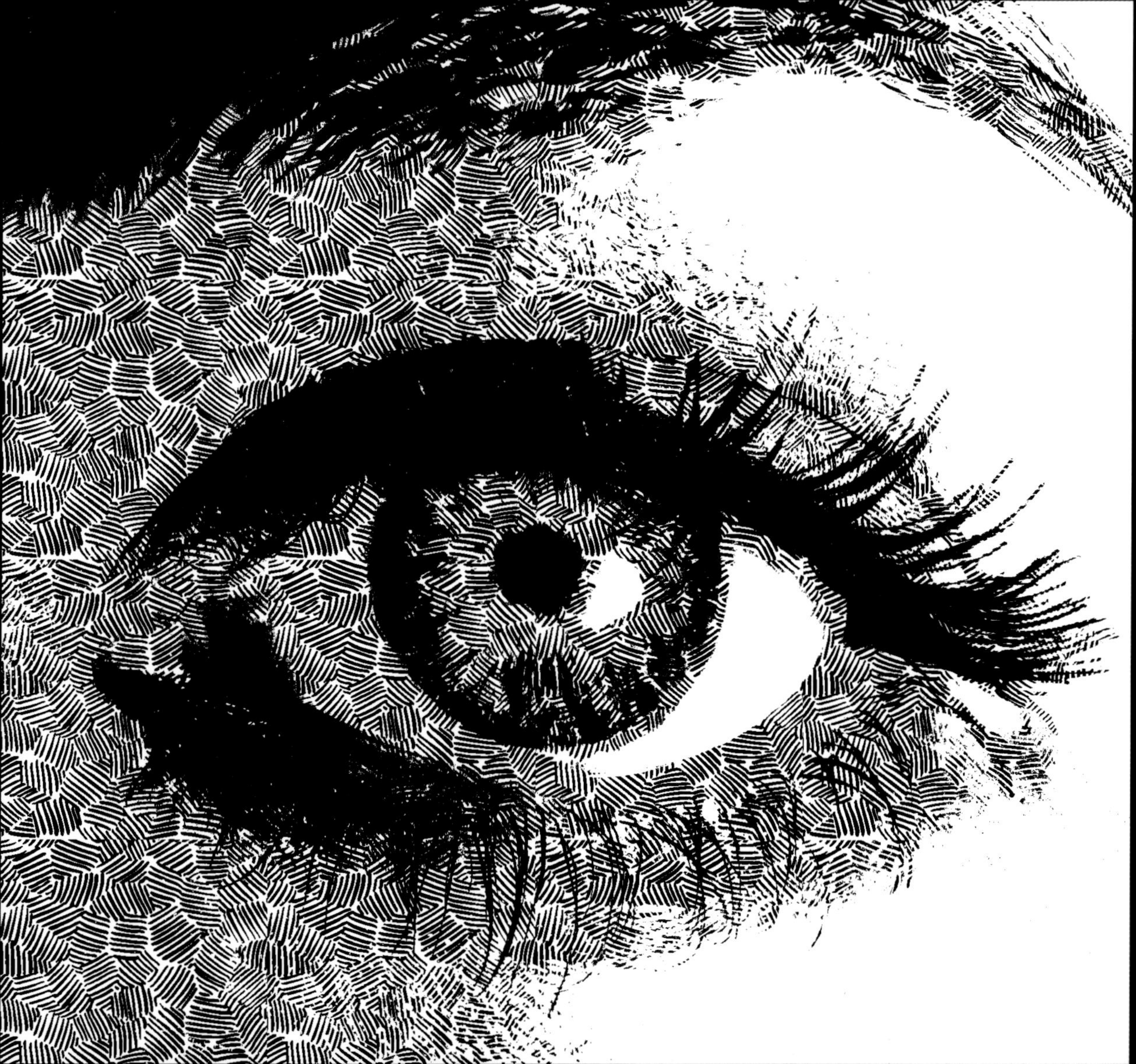

Wrinkled Texture

Layout Program   Resolution: **220** dpi

Scan Program   Size: **1.89** MB

Graphics Program   Difficulty:

☑ Digital Imaging

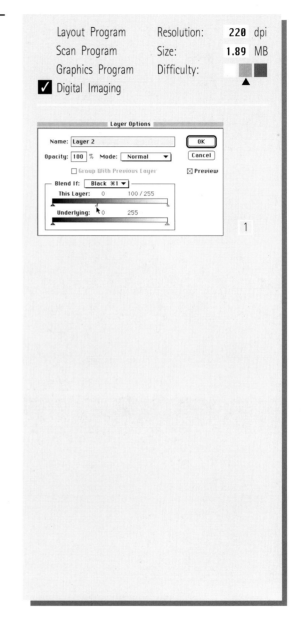

- Scan a crumpled piece of paper in black and white. Make the file the same size and resolution as the original halftone.

- Open the scan in Photoshop. (⌘**O** or F**ile**)

- Open the original halftone in Photoshop. (⌘**O** or **File**)

- Combine the scan and the original halftone:
  Use the Move tool to drag the original halftone onto the scan. *A new layer is generated containing the original image.*

- Modify the transparency of the original image:
  Double-click on the image layer thumbnail to open the Layer Options dialog box. 1
  > This Layer: Hold down the option key and drag the left hand side of the white slider.
  > *This controls which pixel values are blended.*

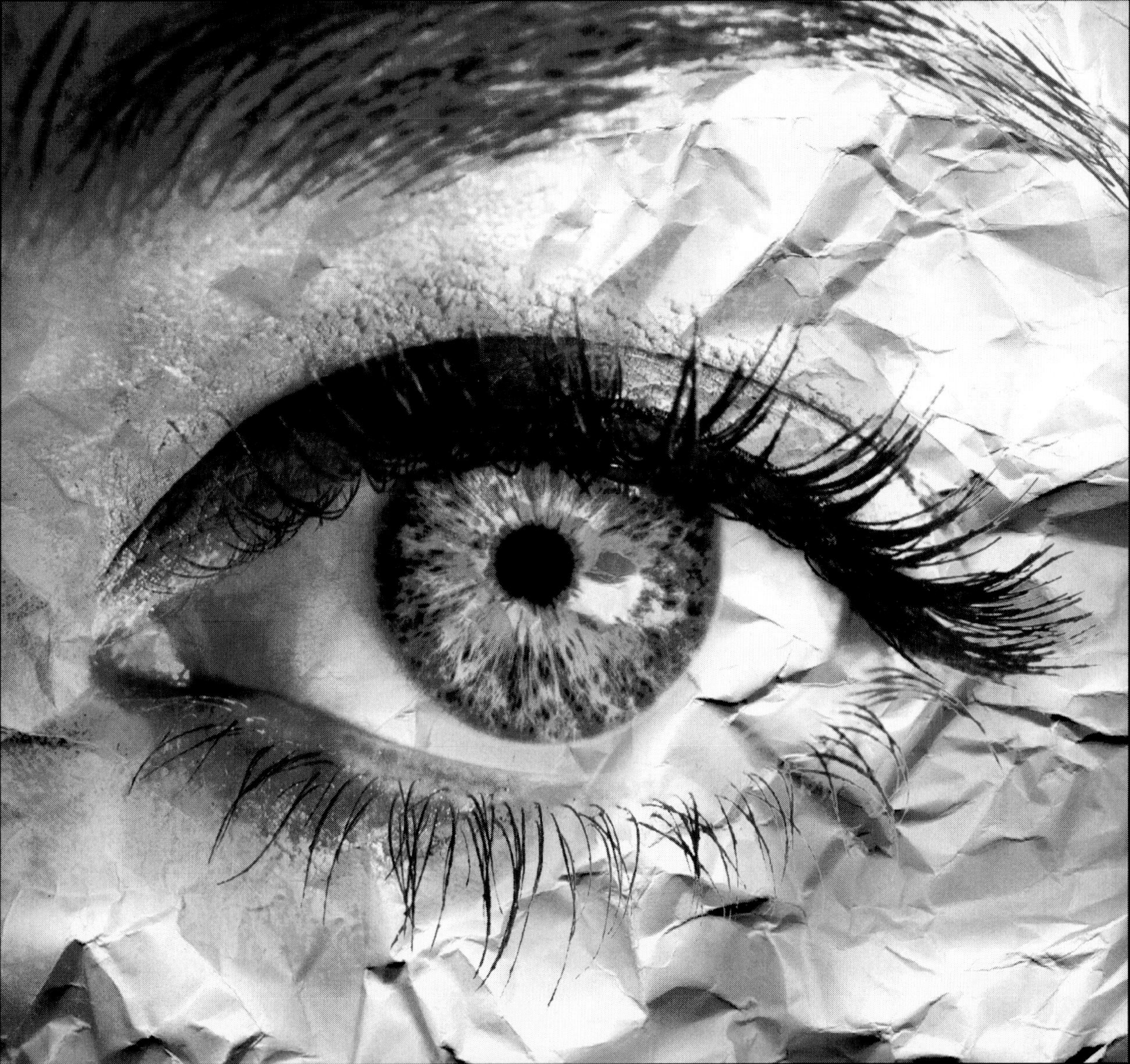

Wrinkled Line Art

- Open the original halftone in FreeHand as a TIFF.
  (⌘**O** or **File**)

- Open the Inspector Palette. (⌘**I** or **Window**)
  Choose the Object Inspector.
  Click the Edit button.
  Adjust the contrast. 1

- Scan a crumpled piece of paper. Make the file the same size
  and resolution as the original halftone.
  Place the image in FreeHand. (⌘ **shift D** or **File**)

- Position the scan over the original image.
  Choose Transparent on the Object Inspector for the scanned
  image. 2

- Clone the transparent wrinkled paper image.
  (⌘**=** or **Edit>Clone**)

- Change the fill color to white:
  Drag the white swatch from the Color List and drop it on
  the Fill Selector. 3

- Offset the scanned image slightly using the Move tool.

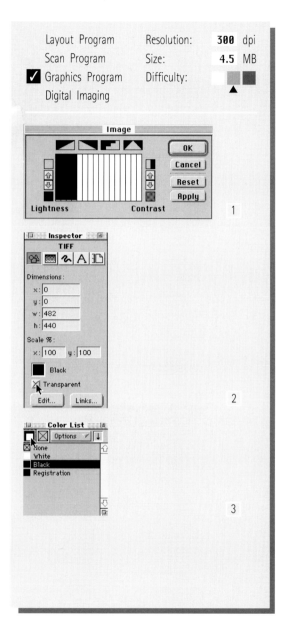

Layout Program
Scan Program
✓ Graphics Program
Digital Imaging

Resolution: **300** dpi
Size: **4.5** MB
Difficulty:

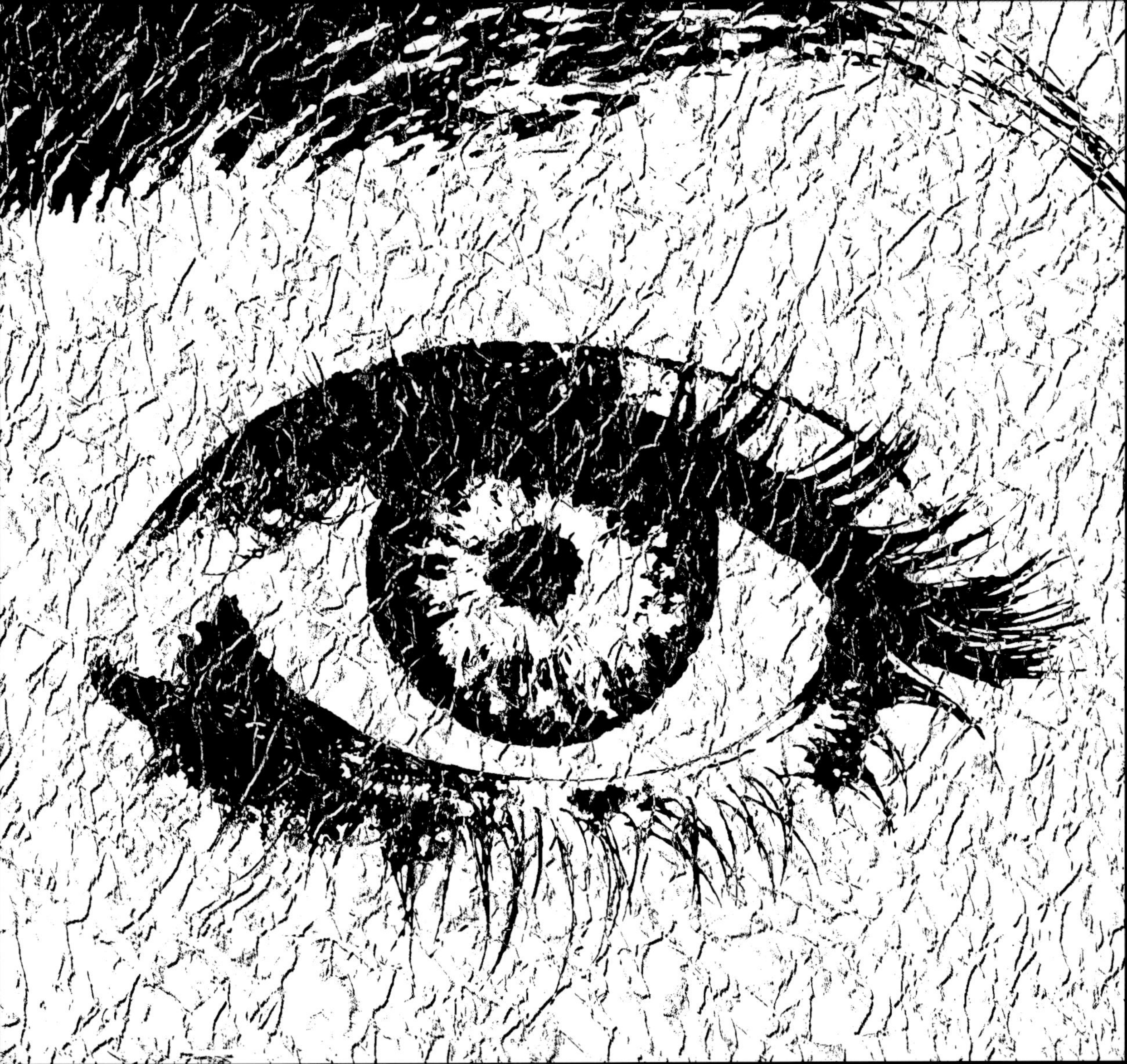

Type as Image

- Create a file of black type within a PostScript drawing program such as Illustrator or FreeHand.
  Make it the same size as your halftone original.
  Save it as an EPS file. (⌘S or **File**)
  Name it "Text."

- Open the original halftone in Photoshop. (⌘O or **File**)

- Open the Brightness/Contrast dialog box.
  (⌘B or **Image>Adjust**) 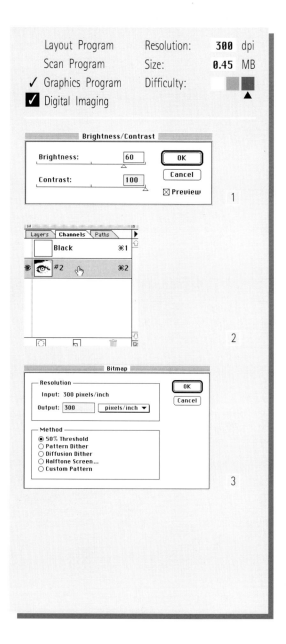1
      Brightness: 60   Contrast: 100

- Select All (⌘A or **Select**) and Cut (⌘X or **Edit**) the image.

- Open the Channels palette. (**Window>Palettes**) 2
  Create a new Channel.
  Paste the halftone into the Channel. (⌘V or **Edit**)

- Open the file "Text." (⌘O or **File**)
  Select All (⌘A or **Select**) and Copy (⌘C or **Edit**) the type.

- Return to the image file.
  Target the Black Channel.
  Paste the text into the Channel. (⌘V or **Edit**)

- Invert the image. (⌘I or **Image>Map**)

- Use the Load Selection command to load the saved selection. (**Select**)

- Invert the image. (⌘I or **Image>Map**)

- Select the Bitmap mode option. (**Mode**) 3
      Output: 300 pixels/inch
      Method: 50% Threshold

Layout Program   Resolution: **300** dpi
Scan Program   Size: **0.45** MB
✓ Graphics Program   Difficulty:
✓ Digital Imaging

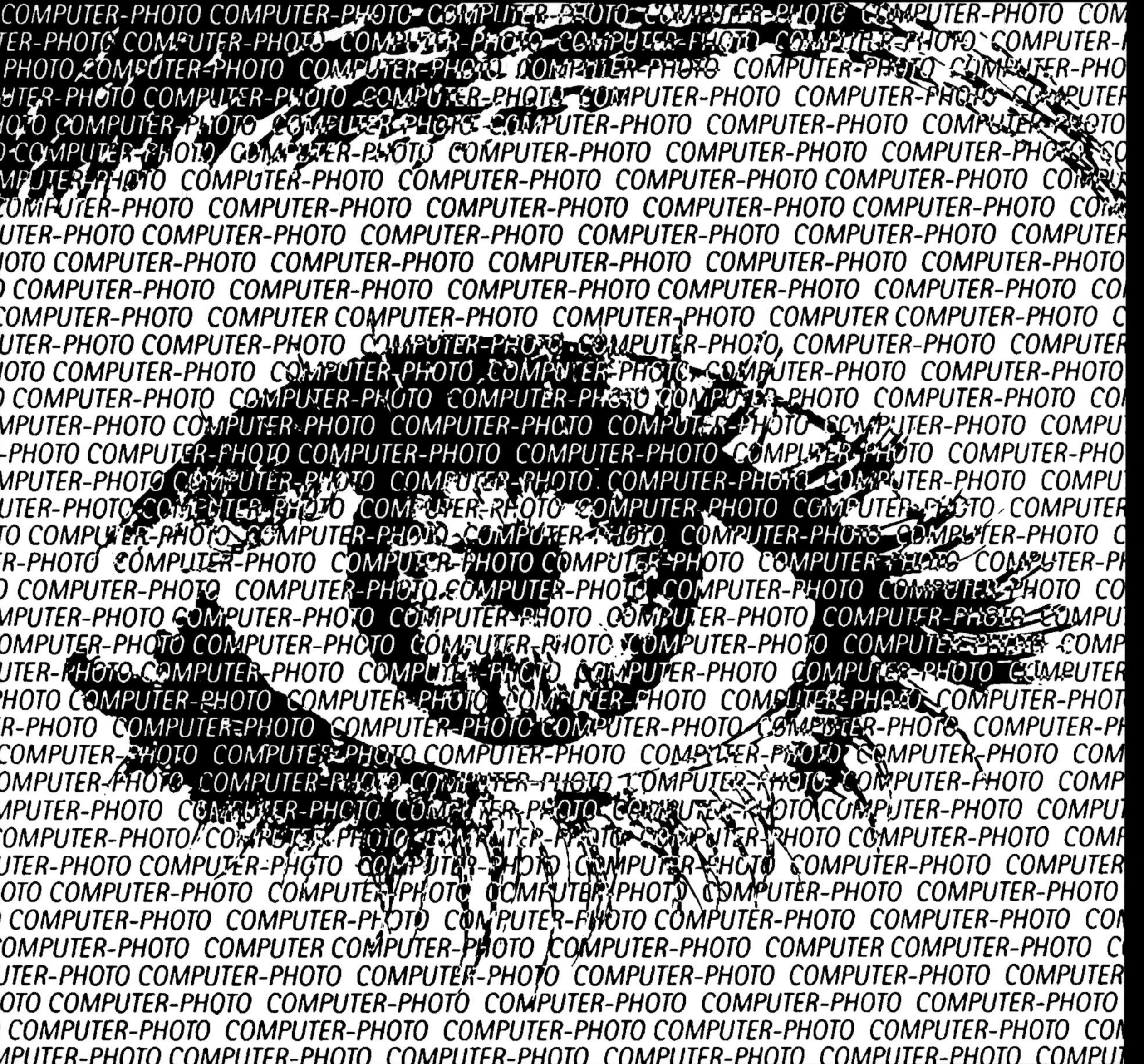
COMPUTER-PHOTO

Earth Texture

- Open the original halftone in Photoshop. (**⌘O** or **File**)

- Open the Brightness/Contrast dialog box.
  (**⌘B** or **Image>Adjust**)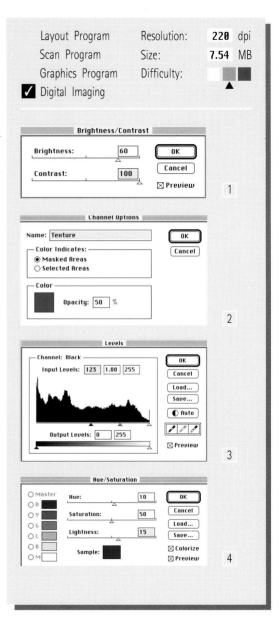
    Brightness: 60   Contrast: 100

- Select All (**⌘A** or **Select**) and Copy (**⌘C** or **Edit**) the image.

- Scan an image of parched earth in black and white.
  Make sure this file is the same size and resolution as the original halftone.
  Open the scan in Photoshop. (**⌘O** or **File**)

- Open the Channels palette. (**Window>Palettes**)
  Create a new Channel. Open the Channel Options dialog box. 2
  Name it "Texture."   Opacity: 50%
  Paste the image from the Clipboard. (**⌘V** or **Edit**)

- Target the Black Channel.
  Use the Load Selection command to load the saved selection. (**Select**)

- Invert the image. (**⌘I** or **Image>Map**)

- Open the Levels dialog box. (**⌘L** or **Image>Adjust**) 3
    Input Levels:
    Black: 123   Gamma: 1.00   White: 255

- Select the CMYK mode option. (**Mode**)

- Open the Hue/Saturation dialog box.
  (**⌘U** or **Image>Adjust**) 4
  Select Colorize and use the sliders to adjust the image.
    Hue: 10   Saturation: 50   Lightness: 15

Layout Program	Resolution:	220	dpi
Scan Program	Size:	7.54	MB
Graphics Program	Difficulty:		
✔ Digital Imaging			

SOLARIZATIONS

Solarization effects can be created in the photographic lab by inverting tonal values from the positive to the negative. Such solarization effects can also be generated on computers by swapping and shifting tonal values.

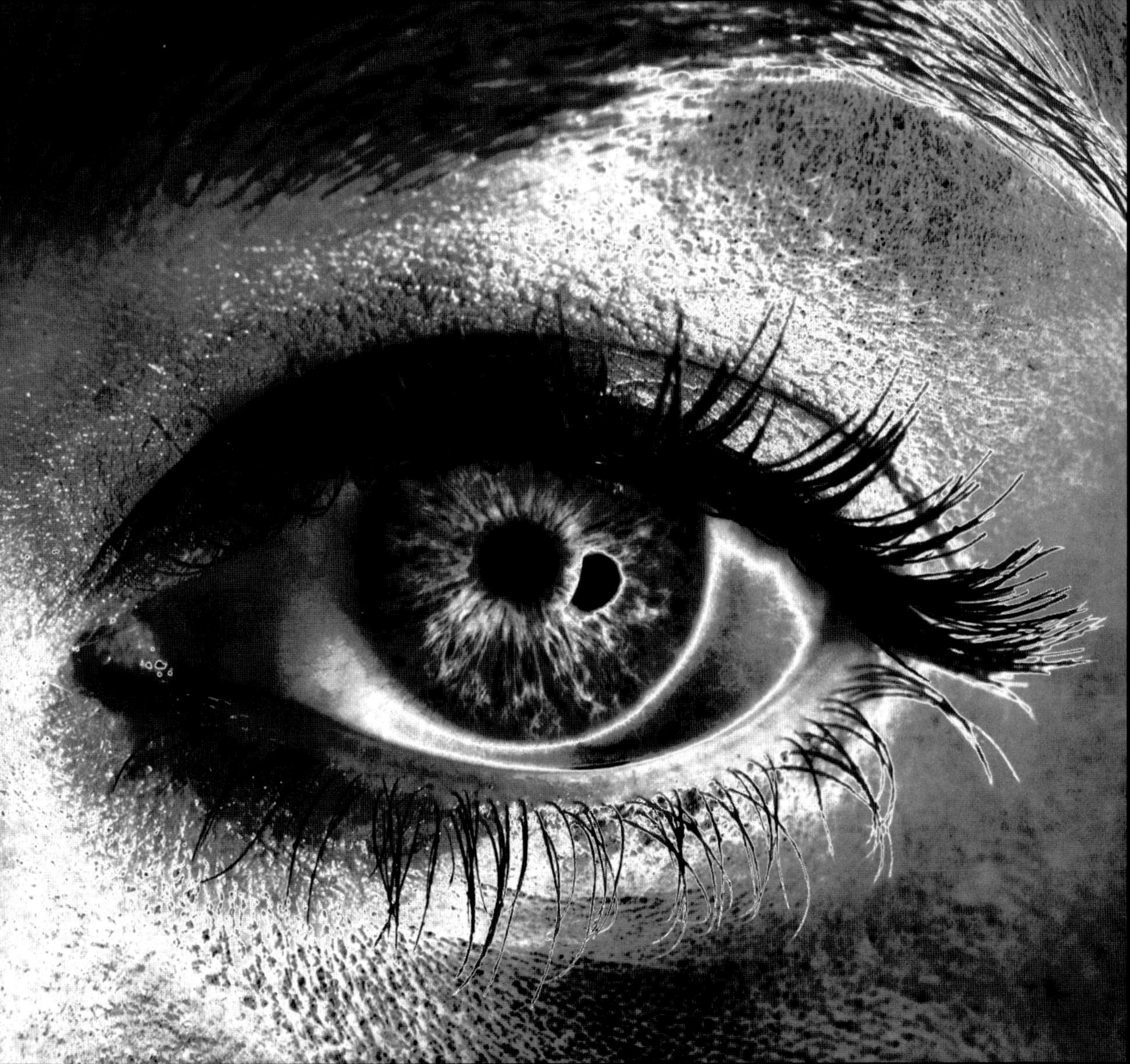

Pseudo Solarization

Layout Program   Resolution: **220** dpi
Scan Program   Size: **2.3** MB
☑ Graphics Program   Difficulty:
Digital Imaging

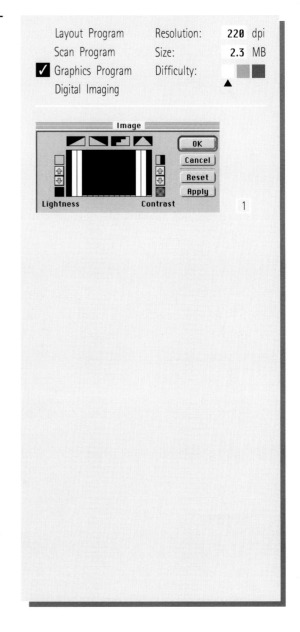

- Open the original image in FreeHand as a TIFF.
  (⌘**O** or **File**)

- Open the Inspector Palette. (⌘**I** or **Window**)
  Choose the Object Inspector.
  Click the Edit button.
  Adjust the 2nd, 3rd, 14th and 15th bars.   1
  Click OK.

▶ *Page 87 (Chapter Title Page): Solarization*
Open the original halftone in Photoshop. (⌘**O** *or* **File**)
Apply the Solarize filter. (**Filter>Stylize**)
Apply the Auto Levels command to the solarized image.
(**Image>Adjust**)

Tonal Composites

- Open the original image in FreeHand as a TIFF. (⌘O or **File**)

- Open the Inspector Palette. (⌘I or **Window**)
  Choose the Object Inspector.
  Click the Edit button.
  Adjust the contrast.

- Create a Clone of your image. (⌘= or **Edit>Clone**)

- Target the Object Inspector.
  Choose Transparent for the copied image.
  Click the Edit button. 1
  Increase the image contrast.

- Change the fill color to white:
  Drag the white swatch from the Color List and drop it on the Fill Selector. 2

- Create a Clone of your image. (⌘= or **Edit>Clone**)

- Target the Object Inspector.
  Click the Edit button. 3
  Increase the image contrast.

- Change the fill color to black:
  Drag the black swatch from the Color List and drop it on the Fill Selector.

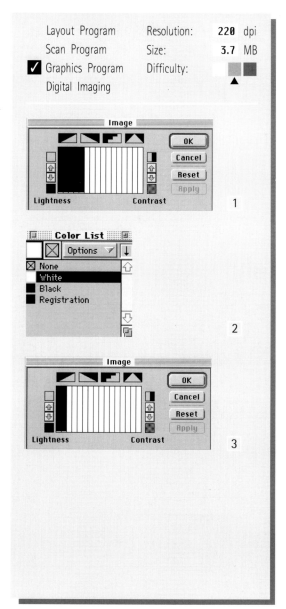

Layout Program — Resolution: **220** dpi
Scan Program — Size: **3.7** MB
☑ Graphics Program — Difficulty:
Digital Imaging

Colored Solarization

- Open the original halftone in Photoshop. (⌘O or **File**)
- Select the RGB mode option. (**Mode**)
- Open the Curves dialog box   (⌘M or **Image>Adjust**)
       Channel: Red (⌘1) 1

  Click on the curve and adjust it accordingly.
  *Altering the Red Channel tints the image and
  automatically shifts the Green and Blue Channel
  curves.*

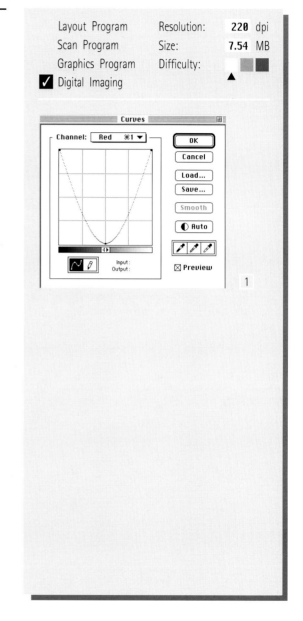

Layout Program	Resolution:	220 dpi
Scan Program	Size:	7.54 MB
Graphics Program	Difficulty:	
✓ Digital Imaging		

Color Bleed

- Open the original halftone in Photoshop. (⌘O or **File**)

- Select the RGB mode option. (**Mode**)
  Select the Indexed Colors mode option. (**Mode**)

- Open the Color Table dialog box. (**Mode**) 1
     Table: Grayscale
  Select a group of squares (values).
  Choose a first color from the Color Picker. 2
  Choose a last color from the Color Picker. 3

- Repeat the process for additional grayscale ranges.

To create a solarization effect, select darker colors for the lighter gray areas and lighter colors for the darker gray areas.

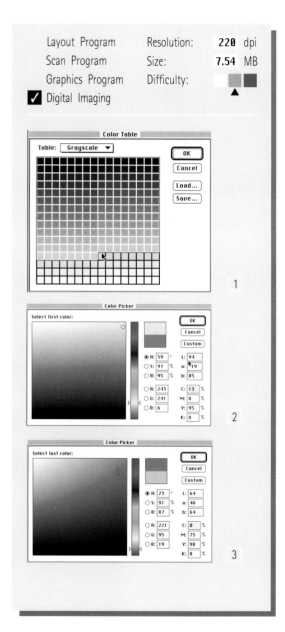

Layout Program
Scan Program
Graphics Program
✓ Digital Imaging

Resolution: **220** dpi
Size: **7.54** MB
Difficulty:

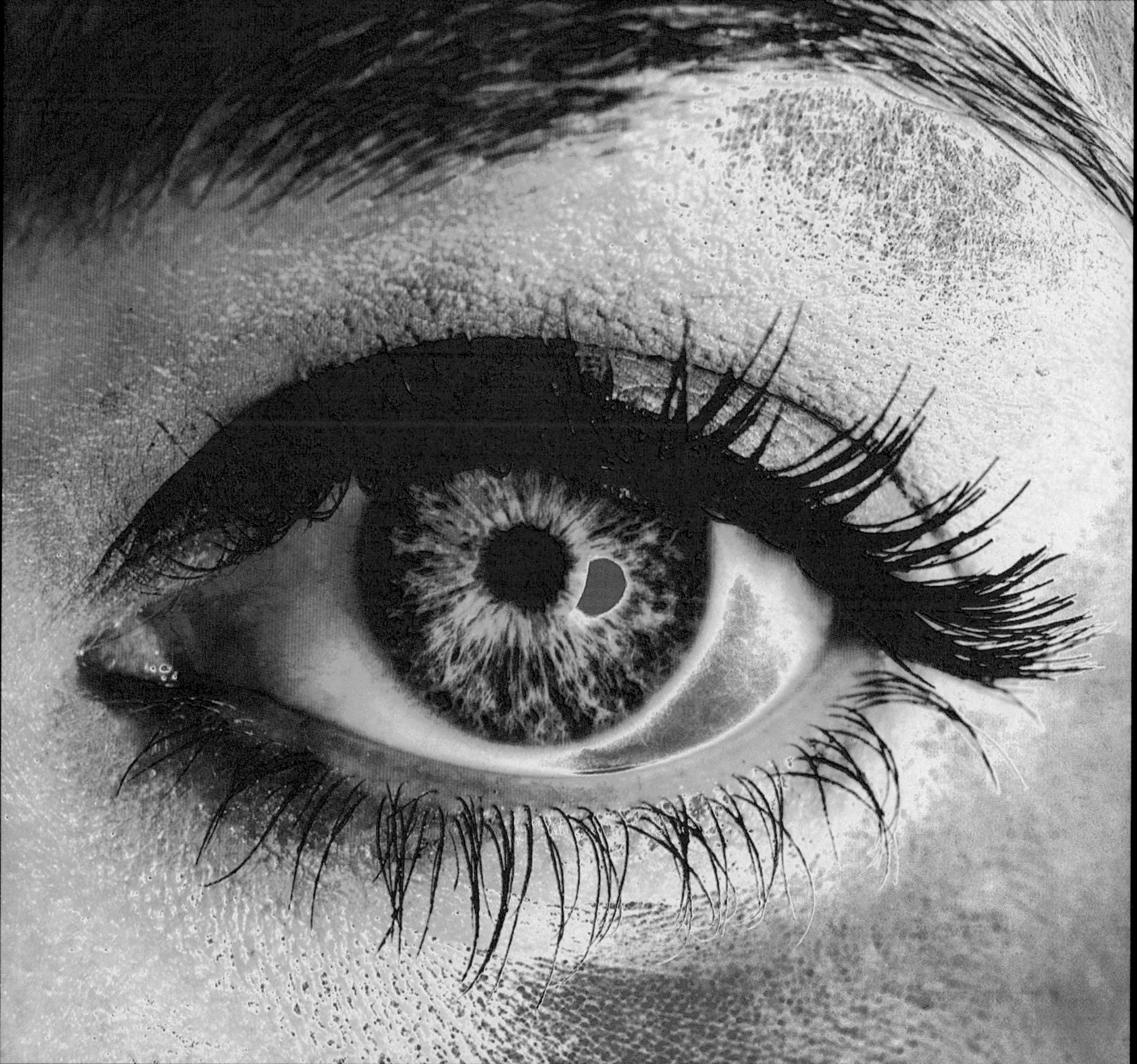

COLORIZATIONS

Colorizing black-and-white images on the computer uses principally the same technique as chemical colorization methods. Either the black image areas are converted into colors and the white background remains the same, or vice versa. Using various combinations of these techniques can substantially increase the effectiveness of black-and-white subjects.

Monochromatic Colorization

- Open the original halftone in Photoshop. (⌘O or **File**)

- Select the RGB mode option. (**Mode**)

- Select a Foreground color:
  Click on the Foreground color swatch or select a color from the Swatch palette.

- Apply a Fill. (**Edit**) 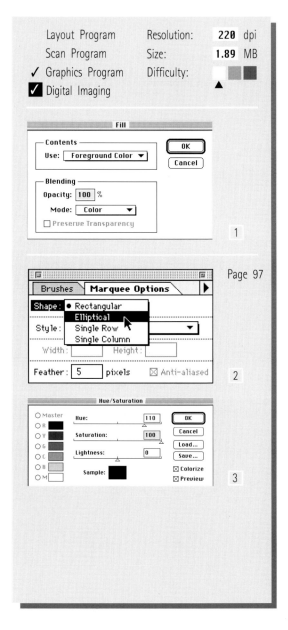 1
  Shortcut: Shift & Delete opens the Fill dialog box.
      Use: Foreground Color
      Opacity: 100%
      Paint mode: Color

▶ *Page 97 (Chapter Title Page): Selective Colorization*
*Open the original halftone in Photoshop. (⌘O or **File**)*
*Select the CMYK mode option. (**Mode**)*
Double-click on the Marquee tool. 2
      Shape: Elliptical
      Feather: 5 pixels
Use the Marquee tool to select the iris of the eye.
Open the Hue/Saturation dialog box (⌘U or
Image>Adjust) 3
Select Colorize and use the sliders to adjust the color.

Layout Program   Resolution: **220** dpi
Scan Program   Size: **1.89** MB
✓ Graphics Program Difficulty:
☑ Digital Imaging   ▲

Fill
┌ Contents ──────────┐   ┌──OK──┐
  Use: [Foreground Color ▼] ┌─Cancel─┐
┌ Blending ──────────┐
  Opacity: [100] %
  Mode: [Color ▼]
  ☐ Preserve Transparency

1

Page 97

[Brushes \ **Marquee Options** \ ▶]
Shape: [● Rectangular]
        [Elliptical]
Style: [Single Row] ▼
        [Single Column]
Width: [   ]   Height: [   ]
Feather: [5] pixels ☒ Anti-aliased

2

Hue/Saturation
○ Master   Hue: [110]   ┌──OK──┐
○ R   ┌─Cancel─┐
○ Y   Saturation: [100] ┌─Load...─┐
○ G   Lightness: [0]   ┌─Save...─┐
○ C
○ B   Sample: ☒ Colorize
○ M   ☒ Preview

3

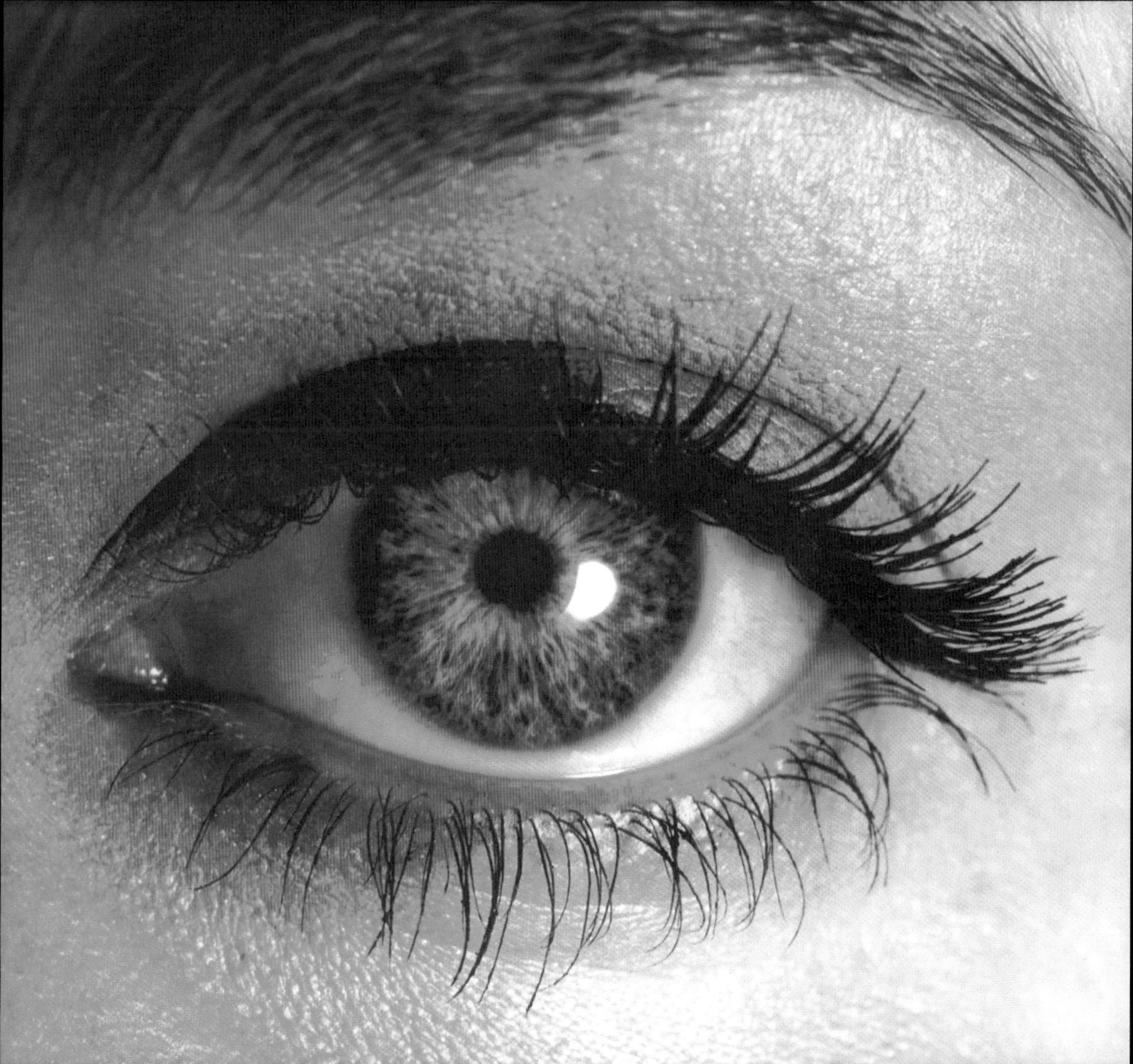

Colorizing Halftones as Line Art

- Open the original image in FreeHand as a TIFF.
  (⌘O or **File**)

- Select the entire image. (⌘A or **Edit**)

- Colorize the image:
  Drag a new color swatch from the Color Mixer
  to the Color List. 1
  Drag the color swatch from the Color List and drop it on
  the Fill Selector or the image itself. 2

- Create a Clone of your image. (⌘= or **Edit**)

- Change the fill color to black:
  Drag the black swatch from the Color List and drop it on
  the Fill Selector.

- Open the Inspector palette. (⌘I or **Window**)
  Choose the Object Inspector.
  Choose Transparent for the copied image.
  Click the Edit button.
  Increase the image contrast. 3

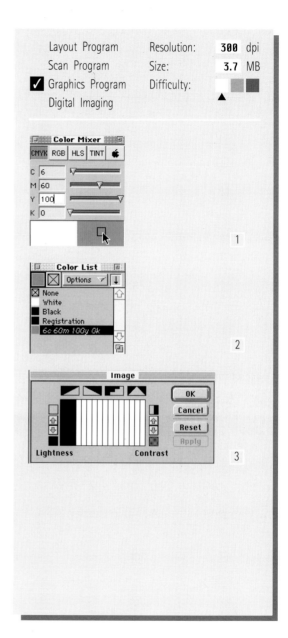

Layout Program Resolution: **300** dpi
Scan Program Size: **3.7** MB
☑ Graphics Program Difficulty:
Digital Imaging

Colorizing Halftones

- Open the original halftone in Photoshop. (**⌘O** or **File**)

- Select the RGB mode option. (**Mode**)

- Open the Brightness/Contrast dialog box.
  (**⌘B** or **Image>Adjust**) 1
  - Brightness: 0
  - Contrast: 20

- Select Yellow for a Foreground color:
  Click on the Foreground Color swatch on the Toolbox.
  Define the color as:
  - C: 0%   M: 0%   Y: 100%   K: 0%

- Apply a Fill. (**Edit**) 2
  Shortcut: Shift & Delete opens the Fill dialog box.
  - Use: Foreground Color
  - Opacity: 100%
  - Mode: Difference

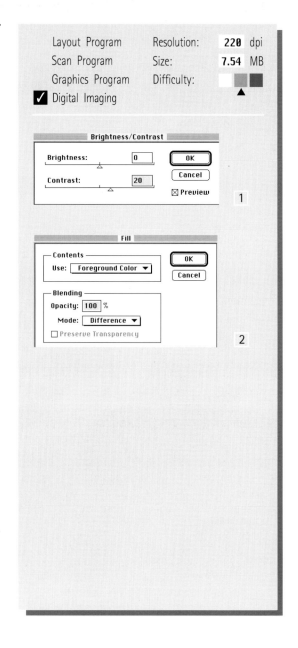

Layout Program   Resolution: **220** dpi
Scan Program   Size: **7.54** MB
Graphics Program   Difficulty:
✓ Digital Imaging

Brightness/Contrast
Brightness: 0
Contrast: 20
OK
Cancel
☒ Preview

1

Fill
Contents
Use: Foreground Color ▼
OK
Cancel
Blending
Opacity: 100 %
Mode: Difference ▼
☐ Preserve Transparency

2

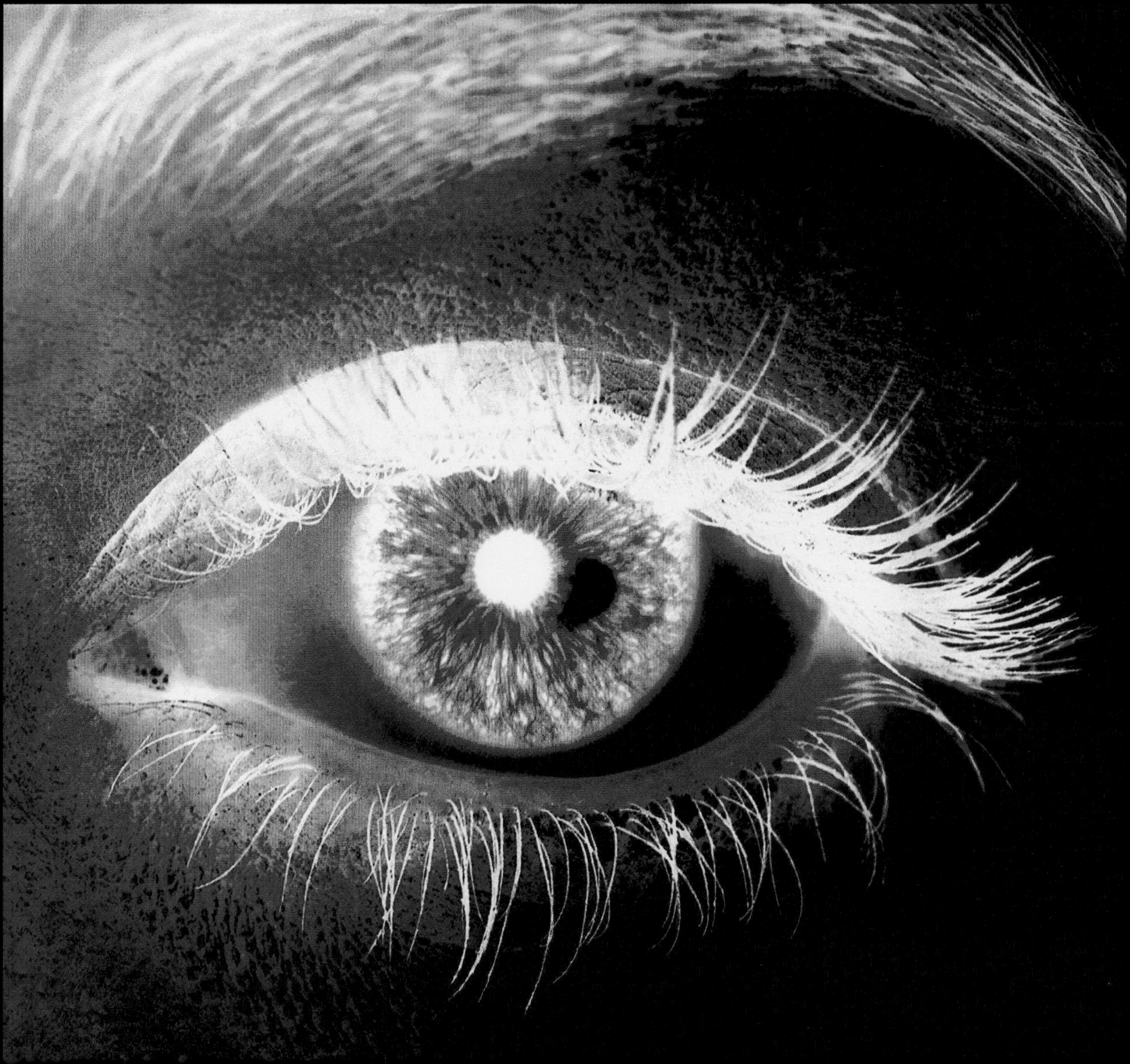

Spectral Colorizing

- Open the original halftone in Photoshop. (⌘O or **File**)

- Select the CMYK mode option. (**Mode**)

- Click on the Foreground Color swatch on the Toolbox. 1
  Define the color as:
       C: 0%   M: 100%   Y: 100%   K: 0%

- Click on the Background Color swatch on the Toolbox. 2
  Define the color as:
       C: 0%   M: 80%   Y: 100%   K: 0%

- Double-click on the Gradient tool. 3
       Paint mode: Color   Opacity: 100%
       Style: Clockwise Spectrum
       Midpoint Skew: 50%
       Type: Linear   Check Dither.
  Click and drag from the top of the image to the bottom.
  This creates a vertical gradient over the whole image.

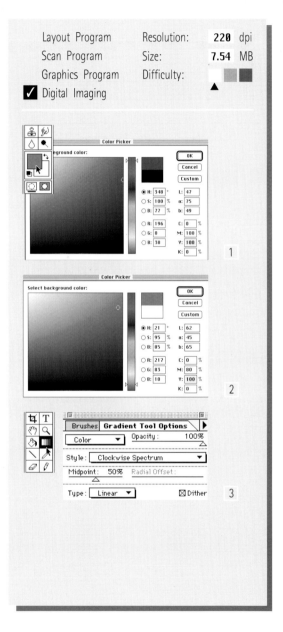

Layout Program	Resolution:	220	dpi
Scan Program	Size:	7.54	MB
Graphics Program	Difficulty:		
✓ Digital Imaging			

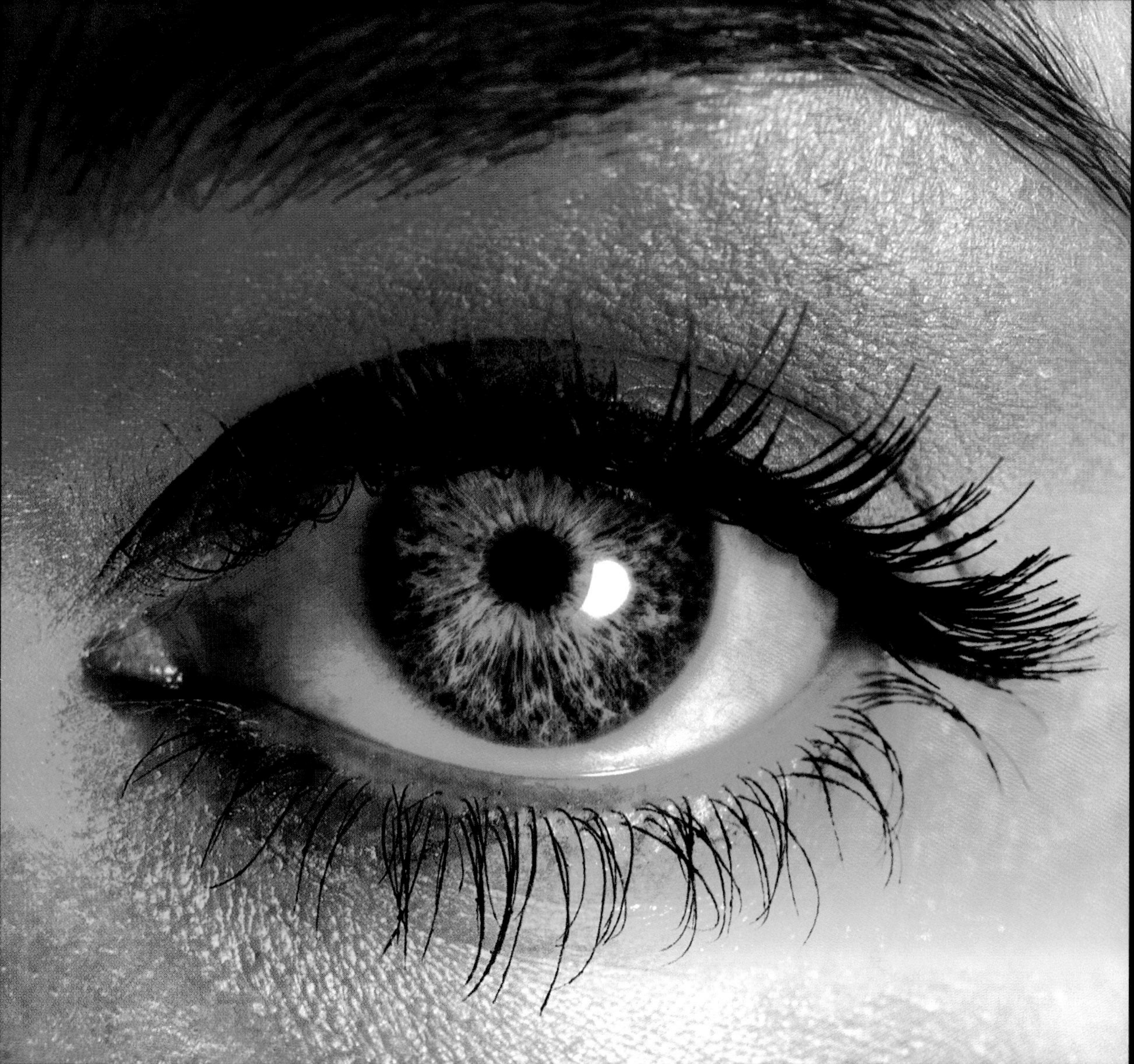

Color Gradients

- Open the original halftone in Photoshop. (**⌘O** or **File**)
- Select the CMYK mode option. (**Mode**)
- Use the rectangular Marquee tool to select the right third of the image.
- Apply Feather to the selection. (**Select**)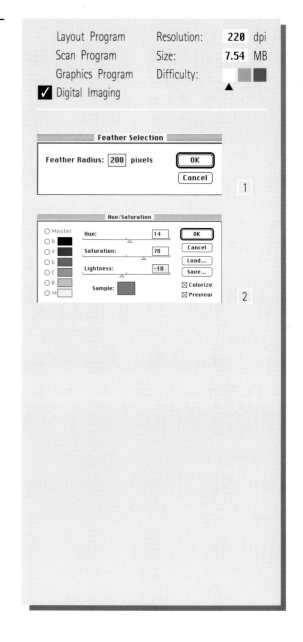
    Radius: 200 pixels
- Open the Hue/Saturation dialog box.
  (**⌘U** or **Image>Adjust**) 2
  Select Colorize and use the sliders to adjust the image.
    Hue: 14
    Saturation: 70
    Lightness: -10

Layout Program
Scan Program
Graphics Program
✓ Digital Imaging

Resolution: **220** dpi
Size: **7.54** MB
Difficulty:
▲

Feather Selection

Feather Radius: 200 pixels   OK
                                Cancel

1

Hue/Saturation

○ Master   Hue: 14   OK
○ R   Cancel
○ Y   Saturation: 70   Load...
○ G   Save...
○ C   Lightness: -10
○ B   Sample: ⊠ Colorize
○ M   ⊠ Preview

2

Colorizing Grain Screens

- Open the original halftone in Photoshop. (⌘O or **File**)

- Select the Bitmap mode option. (**Mode**)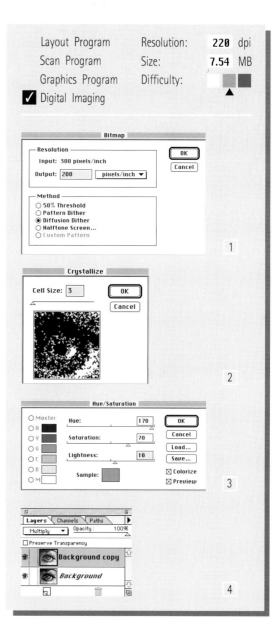
    Output: 200 pixels/inch
    Method: Diffusion Dither

- Select the Grayscale mode option. (**Mode**)

- Apply the Crystallize filter. (**Filter>Stylize**) 2
    Cell Size: 3

- Select the RGB mode option. (**Mode**)

- Open the Layers palette. (**Window>Palettes**)
    Duplicate the Layer.
    Shortcut: drag the current layer onto the New Layer icon.

- Open the Hue/Saturation dialog box.
    (**⌘U** or I**mage>Adjust**) 3
    Select Colorize and use the sliders to adjust the image.
        Hue: 170
        Saturation: 70
        Lightness: 10

- Choose the layer blend mode: Multiply 4
    The Multiply mode multiplies the base color and top color resulting in a darker color.

Layout Program   Resolution: **220** dpi
Scan Program   Size: **7.54** MB
Graphics Program   Difficulty:
☑ Digital Imaging

Fake Duotone

- Open the original halftone in Photoshop. (⌘O or **File**)

- Select the CMYK mode option. (**Mode**)

- Click on the Foreground Color swatch on the Toolbox. 1
  Define the color as:
    C: 0%   M: 0%   Y: 100%   K: 0%

- Select All. (⌘A or **Select**)

- Apply a Fill. (**Edit**) 2
  Shortcut: Shift & Delete opens the Fill dialog box.
      Use: Foreground Color
      Opacity: 100%
      Paint mode: Multiply

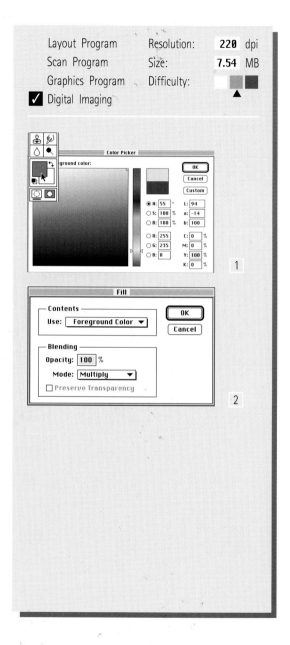

Layout Program   Resolution: **220** dpi
Scan Program   Size: **7.54** MB
Graphics Program   Difficulty:
✓ Digital Imaging

1

2

Duotone

- Open the original halftone in Photoshop. (**⌘0** or **File**)
- Select the Duotone mode option. (**Mode**) 1
    Type: Duotone
    Click on the Ink 2 swatch.
  Select a yellow from the Color Picker as the second color.
  Since this book was printed in a four-color process, the
  choices available for the second color are limited to yellow,
  cyan or magenta. A duotone with a spot color is also
  possible, as long as it is used later in the printing process.
  This color can be selected using the Color Table option in
  the Color Picker.
- Click on the Ink 2 Curve icon. 2
  Modify the additional ink's light/dark distribution in the
  Duotone Curve dialog box.

► Page 114: Tritone
  Same procedure as with Duotone.
      Type: Tritone 3
  Select two additional colors (yellow and cyan) as Ink 2 and
  Ink 3.

► Page 115: Quadtone
  Same procedure as with Duotone and Tritone.
      Type: Quadtone 4
  Select three additional colors (yellow, cyan and magenta)as
  Ink 2, Ink 3 and Ink 4.

Layout Program	Resolution:	220	dpi
Scan Program	Size:	7.54	MB
Graphics Program	Difficulty:		
✓ Digital Imaging			

Duotone Options

Type: Duotone

Ink 1: Black
Ink 2: yellow
Ink 3:
Ink 4:

OK
Cancel
Load...
Save...

Overprint Colors...

1

Duotone Curve

0:	0	%	60:		%
5:		%	70:		%
10:		%	80:		%
20:		%	90:		%
30:		%	95:		%
40:		%	100:	100	%
50:	38.1	%			

OK
Cancel
Load...
Save...

2

Duotone Options

Type: Tritone

Ink 1: Black
Ink 2: yellow
Ink 3: cyan
Ink 4:

OK
Cancel
Load...
Save...

Overprint Colors...

3

Page 114

Duotone Options

Type: Quadtone

Ink 1: Black
Ink 2: yellow
Ink 3: cyan
Ink 4: magenta

OK
Cancel
Load...
Save...

Overprint Colors...

4

Page 115

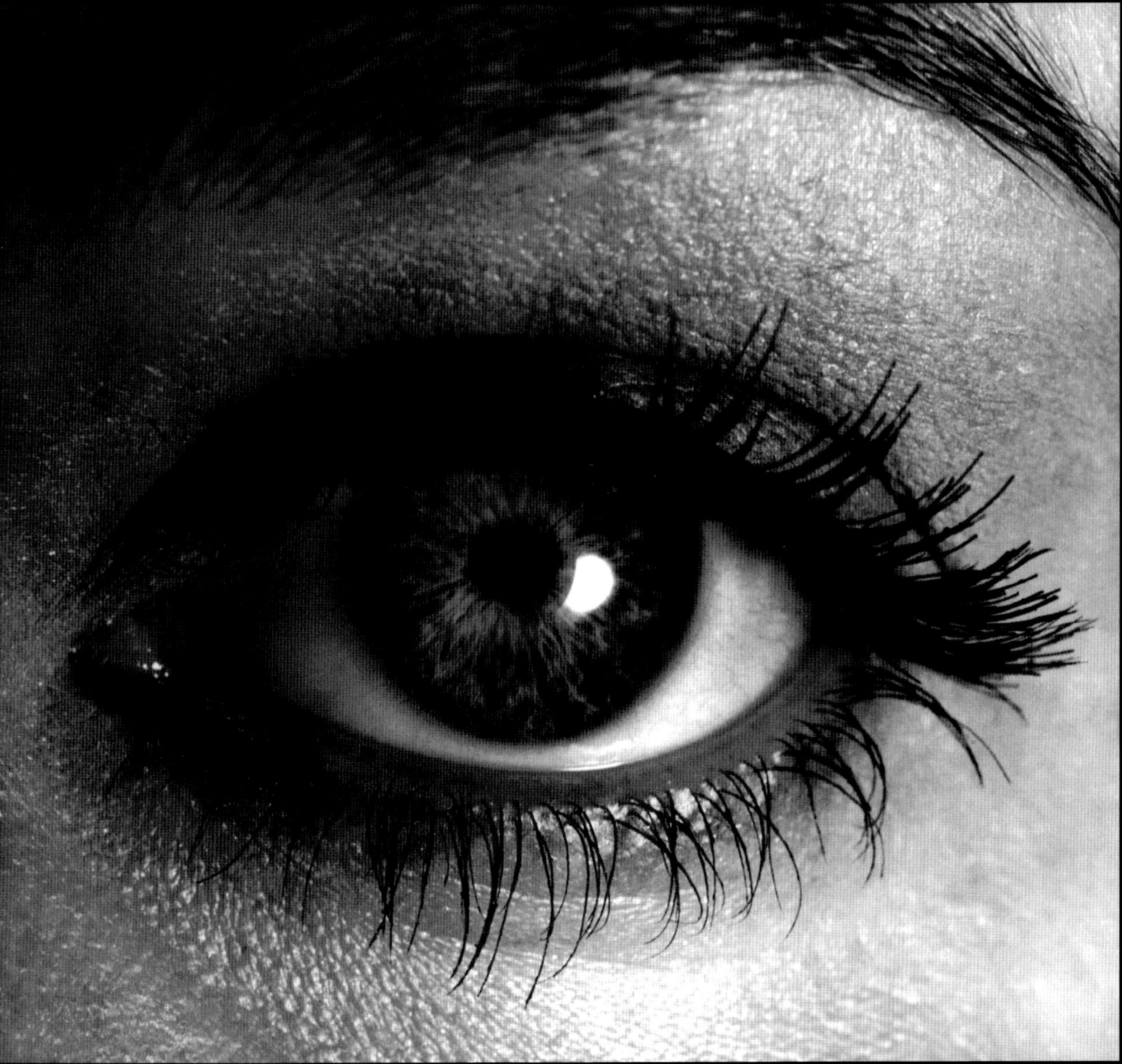

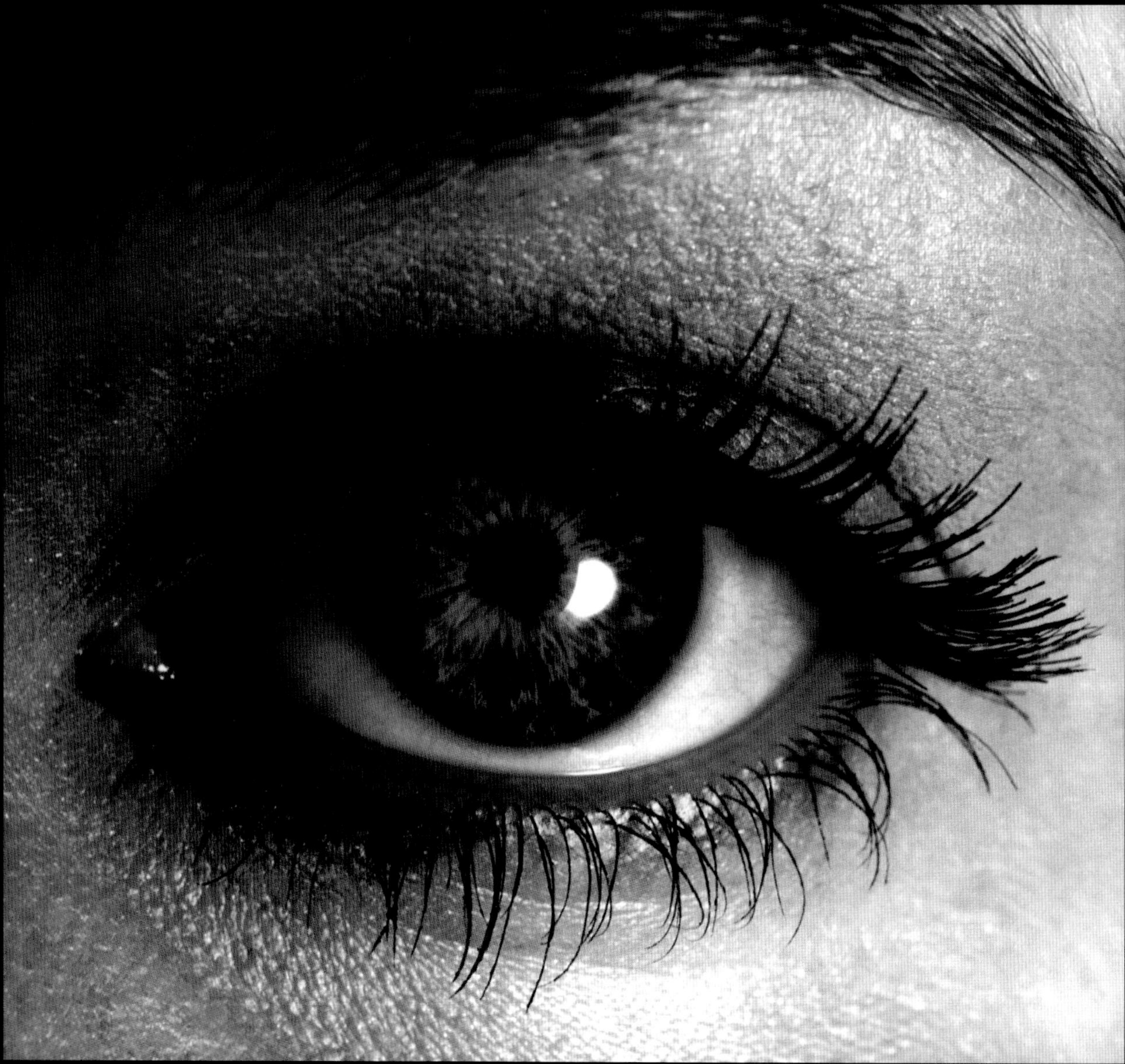

DYNAMIC EFFECTS

The computer offers a wide variety of options for creating motion effects. Expanding the image area, utilizing smudge effects and distortion filters or superimposing various image sizes and combinations of these techniques make the possibilities in this area seem infinite.

Double Distortion

- Open the original halftone in Photoshop. (**⌘O** or **File**)

- Apply the Spherize filter. (**Filter>Distort**) 1
    Amount: -100%
    Mode: Horizontal only

- Apply the filter a second time.
    Shortcut: ⌘F reapplies the last filter.

▶ *Page 119 (Chapter Title Page): High Distortion*
    Open the original halftone in Photoshop. (⌘O or File)
    *Apply the Pinch filter. (**Filter>Distort**) 2*
        Amount: 100%

▶ *Page 122: Spherical Distortion*
    Open the original halftone in Photoshop. (⌘O or File)
    *Apply the Spherize filter. (**Filter>Distort**) 3*
        Amount: -100%
        Mode: Normal

▶ *Page 123: Wave Distortion*
    Open the original halftone in Photoshop. (⌘O or File)
    *Apply the Shear filter. (**Filter>Distort**) 4*
        Undefined Areas: Repeat Edge Pixels
    Create and drag points along the reference line to indicate
    the level of distortion.

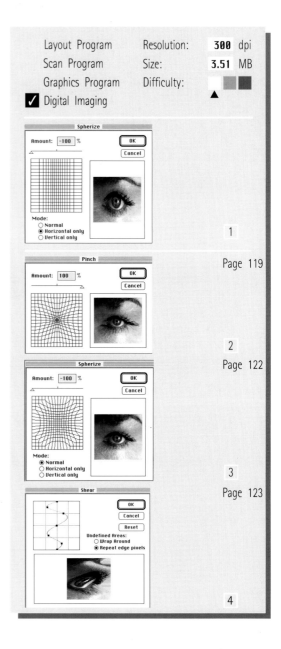

Layout Program	Resolution:	**300** dpi
Scan Program	Size:	**3.51** MB
Graphics Program	Difficulty:	
✓ Digital Imaging		

1

Page 119

2

Page 122

3

Page 123

4

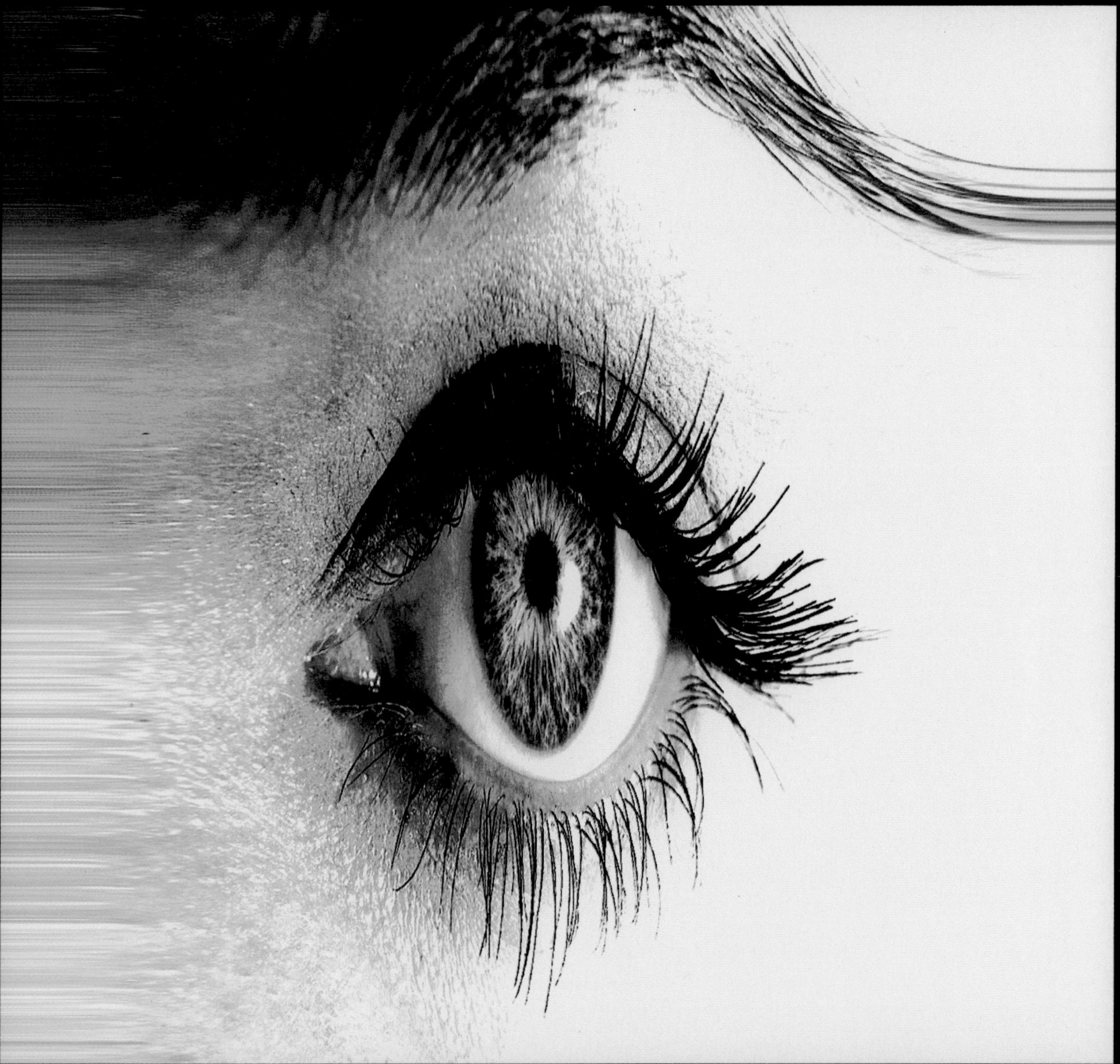

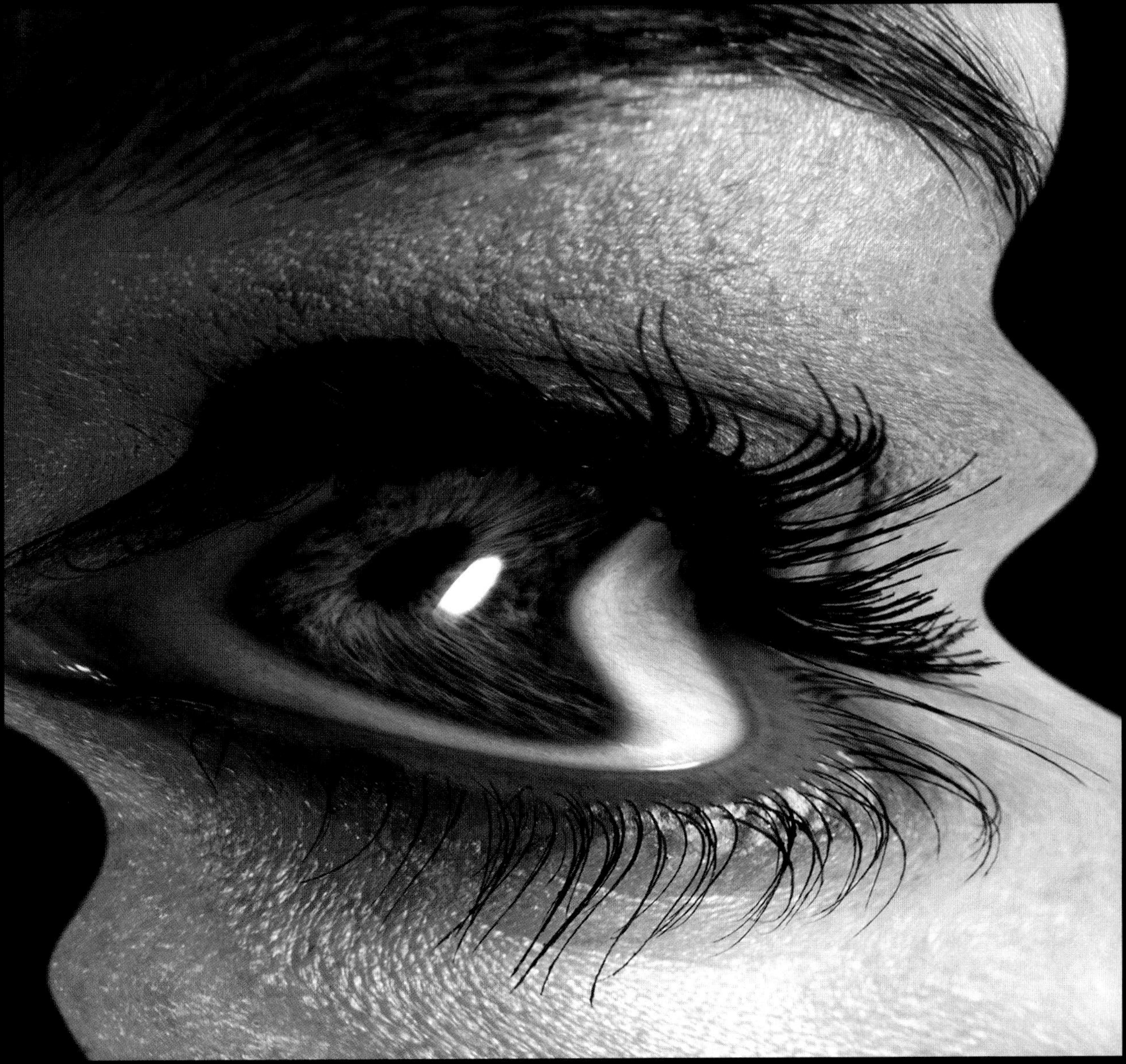

Perspective

Layout Program   Resolution: **300** dpi
Scan Program   Size: **6.3** MB
☑ Graphics Program   Difficulty:
Digital Imaging

- Create a pattern of squares in FreeHand. 1

- Place the original image in FreeHand as a TIFF. (⌘ **shift D** or **File**) Align it on the pattern of squares.

- Colorize the image: Create a new color swatch in the Color Mixer. Drag it from the Color Mixer to the Color List. Drag the new color to the Fill Selector.

- Select All (⌘**A** or **Edit**) and Cut (⌘**X** or **Edit**) the image. Select one of the squares. Paste Inside the original halftone from the Clipboard. (⌘ **Shift V** or **Edit**) Repeat this select and Paste Inside procedure with the rest of the squares.

- Lighten the squares accordingly.

- Place the original image. (⌘ **shift D** or **File**)
  Colorize the image: *(Use instructions above.)*
  Resize the image to fit your pattern.
  Send to back. (⌘**B** or **Item**)

▶*Page 126: Overlay*
*Place the original image in FreeHand as a TIFF. (⌘ **shift D** or **File**) Copy (⌘**C** or **Edit**) the image and Paste (⌘**V** or **Edit**) several images on top of each other. Scale each image down accordingly. Hold down the shift key to constrain proportions.*

▶*Page 127: Perspective Distortion*
*Within FreeHand, create a box the same size as the original halftone. Export it as an EPS file. (⌘**E** or **File**) 2
Open the original halftone in Photoshop. (⌘**O** or **File**)
Select All (⌘**A** or **Select**) and Copy (⌘**C** or **Edit**) the image. Open the exported file in Photoshop. (⌘**O** or **File**)
Paste the original halftone from the clipboard. (⌘**V** or **Edit**)
Select the Skew command. (**Image>Effect**) Grab the corner handles and fit the image into one of the side panels. Repeat the Paste and Skew commands for the remaining surfaces.*

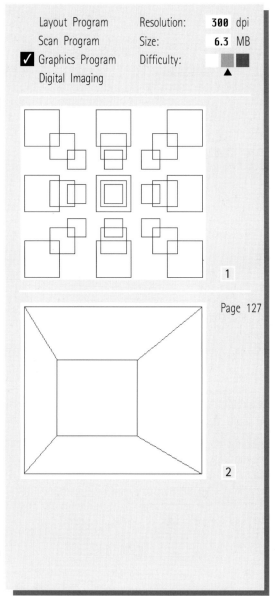

1

Page 127

2

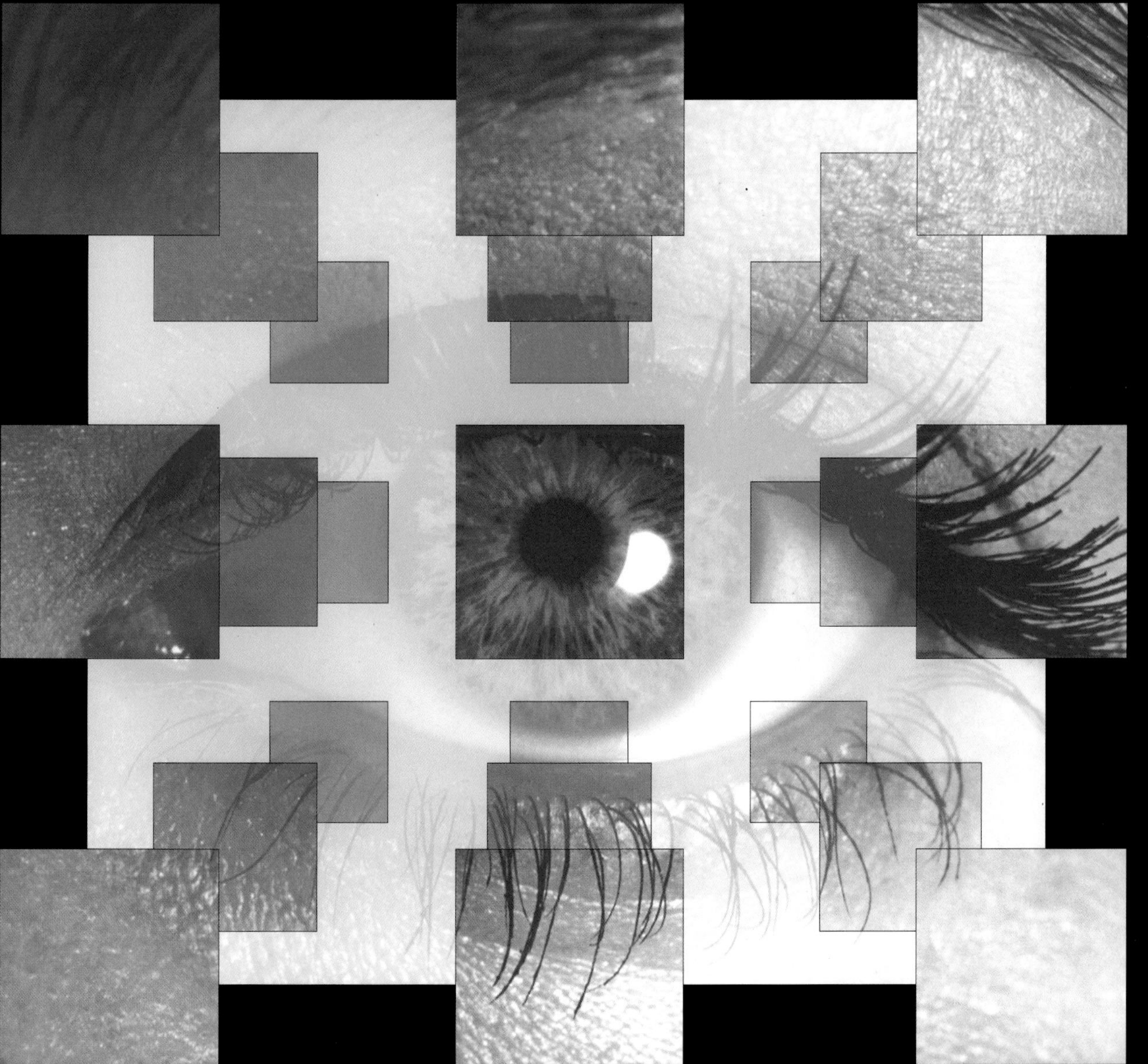

Rotation

- Open the original halftone in Photoshop. (**⌘O** or **File**)
  Set the default Foreground and Background colors.
  Swap the default colors.

- Open the Channels palette. (**Window>Palettes**)
  Create a new channel. Name it "Spiral."
  Set the default colors.
  Use the Line tool to draw a cross in the channel.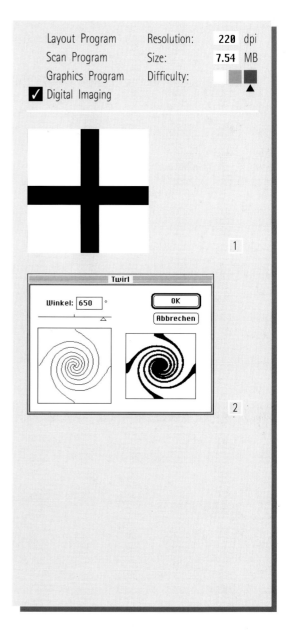
      Line width: 150 pixels

- Apply the Twirl filter. (**Filter>Distort**) 2
      Angle: 650°

- Apply the Gaussian Blur filter. (**Filter>Blur**)
      Radius: 5 pixels

- Target the Black channel.
  Use Load Selection to load the channel "Spiral." (**Select**)
  Open the Curves dialog box. (**⌘M** or **Image>Adjust**)
  Adjust the curve to darken the selection.

- Use the Marquee tool to select a circular area in the middle
  of the eye.
  Apply a Feather. (**Select**)

- Define Black as the background color.
  *Shortcut: Click the Default colors button (D), then the
  Switch colors toggle (X).*
  Delete the selection by pressing the Delete key.

Layout Program	Resolution:	220	dpi
Scan Program	Size:	7.54	MB
Graphics Program	Difficulty:		
✓ Digital Imaging			▲

Perspective Lines

- Create a line pattern in FreeHand the same size as the original halftone. Export the illustration. (**⌘E** or **File**) 1
    Format: Adobe Illustrator® 3

- Open the exported file in Photoshop. (**⌘O** or **File**) Invert the image. (**⌘I** or **Image>Map**)

- Open the original halftone in Photoshop. (**⌘O** or **File**) Select the RGB mode option. (**Mode**)

- Combine the two images: Select the Move tool and drag the line pattern onto the original halftone. Invert the image. (**⌘I** or **Image>Map**)

- Open the Layers palette. (**Window>Palettes**) 2 Choose Lighten as the Layer blend mode. Target the Background Layer. Select a Blue Foreground and Yellow Background color. Click on the respective color swatches and select desired color from the Color Picker.

- Double-click on the Gradient tool. 3
    Mode: Color   Opacity: 50%
    Style: Foreground to Background
    Midpoint Skew: 50%
    Type: Linear   Check Dither.
    Drag from the lower left to the upper right corner of the image.

▶ *Page 132: Motion Blur*
*Open the original halftone in Photoshop. (**⌘O** or **File**)*
*Apply the Motion Blur filter. (**Filter>Blur**)*
    Degrees: 24   Distance: 50
*Apply the Sharpen More filter. (**Filter>Sharpen**)*
*Select the CMYK mode option. (**Mode**) Open the Hue/ Saturation dialog box. (**⌘U** or **Image>Adjust**)*
Select Colorize and use the sliders to adjust the image.

▶ *Page 133: Pyramid Effect*
*Open the original halftone in Photoshop. (**⌘O** or **File**)*
*Apply the Extrude filter. (**Filter>Stylize**)*
    Type: Pyramids   Size: 35 pixels   Depth: 40, Random

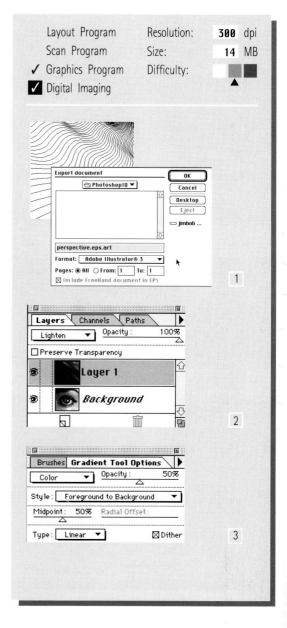

Layout Program	Resolution: **300** dpi
Scan Program	Size: **14** MB
✓ Graphics Program	Difficulty:
✓ Digital Imaging	

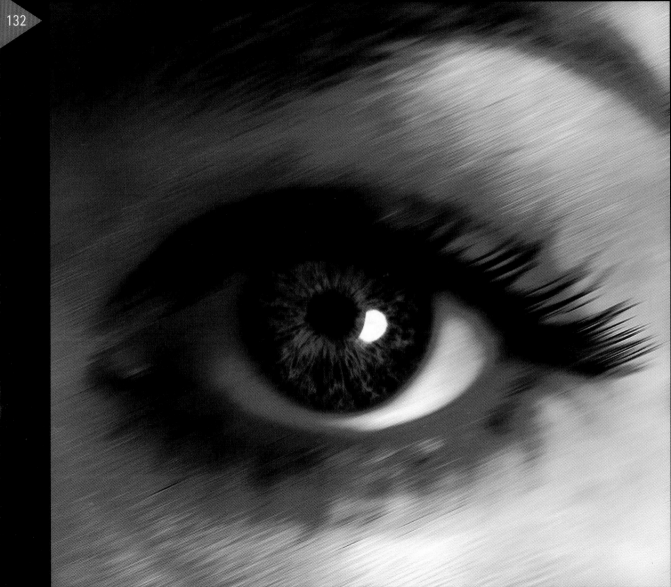

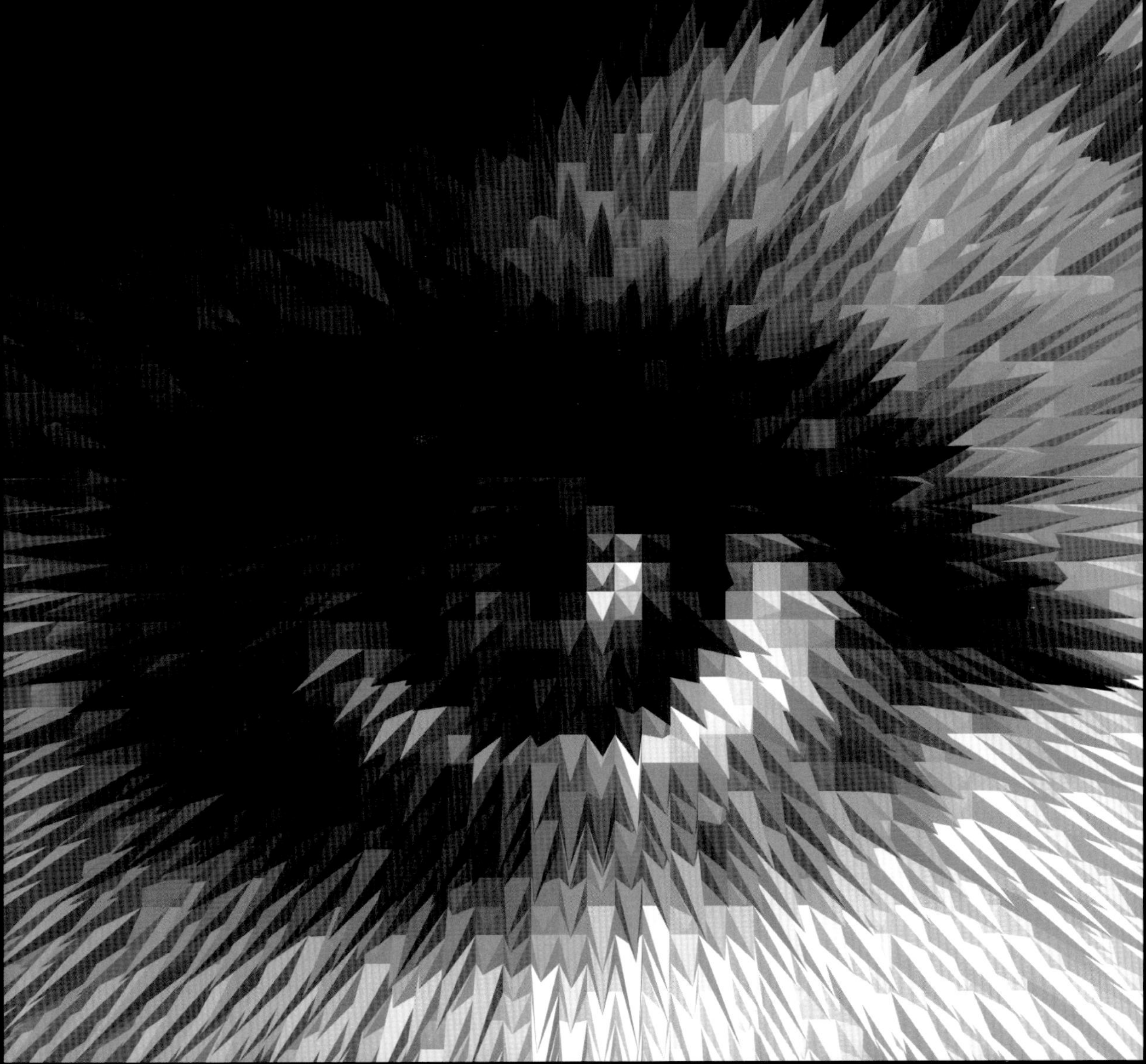

MONTAGES AND MASKS

Combining various image elements into a new image used to require technical know-how and extreme precision. The versatile montage and masking options offered by image manipulation and drawing software packages considerably lighten the task of creating such compositions. The programs allow fast exchanges, shifts, modifications, rotations or combinations of individual elements and thus make creating completely new images easier.

Stencils

- Open the original halftone in Photoshop. (⌘O or **File**)

- Define Black as the background color. 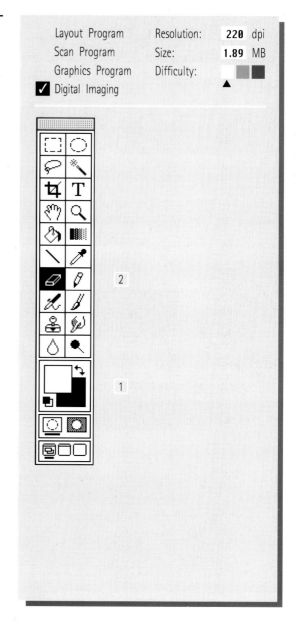 1
  Shortcut: Click the Default colors button (D), then the Switch colors toggle (X).

- Select All (⌘A or **Select**) and Delete.

- Double-click on the Eraser tool in the Toolbox. 2
  - Mode: Paintbrush
  - Opacity: 100%
  - Check Erase to Saved.
  - Click OK. *This erases the black back to the original saved version.*

Note: The Brushes palette also controls the Eraser size.

Layout Program	Resolution:	**220** dpi
Scan Program	Size:	**1.89** MB
Graphics Program	Difficulty:	
✓ Digital Imaging		▲

Reflections

- Open the original halftone in Photoshop. (**⌘O** or **File**)

- Use the Marquee tool to select the left half of the image. Make sure the selection cuts through the center of the pupil.

- Feather the selection. (**Select**) 1
   Radius: 10 pixels

- Float the selection. (**⌘J** or **Select**)

- Apply the Horizontal command. (**Image>Flip**) 2

- Use the Move tool or the arrow keys to match the selected area with its mirror image.

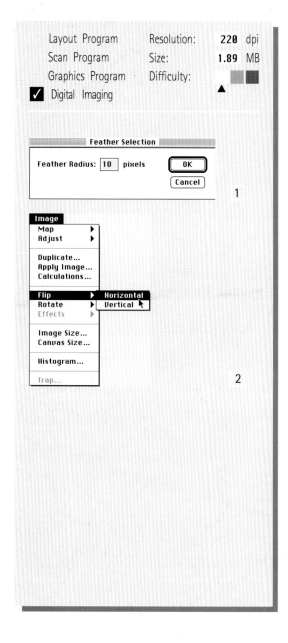

Layout Program   Resolution: **220** dpi
Scan Program   Size: **1.89** MB
Graphics Program   Difficulty:
☑ Digital Imaging

Feather Selection

Feather Radius: 10 pixels   OK   Cancel

1

Image
Map ▶
Adjust ▶

Duplicate...
Apply Image...
Calculations...

Flip ▶   Horizontal
Rotate ▶   Vertical
Effects ▶

Image Size...
Canvas Size...

Histogram...

Trap...

2

Line Art-Halftone Montage

- Open the original halftone in Photoshop. (⌘O or **File**)

- Double-click the Lasso tool. 1
  Feather: 15 pixels   Check Anti-aliased.
  Use the Lasso tool to select an area of the image.
  (In our example, the eyeball.)

- Open the Brightness/Contrast dialog box.
  (**⌘B** or **Image>Adjust**) 2
  Brightness: 0
  Contrast: 95

- Inverse the selection. (**Select**)

- Darken the image midtones slightly:
  Open Levels dialog box. (**⌘L** or **Image>Adjust**) 3
  Decrease the gamma (midtones) Input Levels by moving the
  gamma (middle) slider to the right.

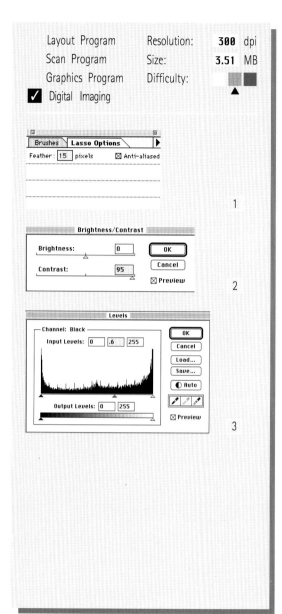

Layout Program   Resolution: **300** dpi
Scan Program   Size: **3.51** MB
Graphics Program   Difficulty:
✓ Digital Imaging

Brushes Lasso Options
Feather: 15 pixels   ☒ Anti-aliased

1

Brightness/Contrast
Brightness: 0   OK
Contrast: 95   Cancel
                      ☒ Preview

2

Levels
Channel: Black
Input Levels: 0 .6 255   OK
                            Cancel
                            Load...
                            Save...
                            ◑ Auto
Output Levels: 0 255   ☒ Preview

3

Combining Subjects

Layout Program   Resolution: **220** dpi
Scan Program   Size: **1.89** MB
Graphics Program   Difficulty:
✓ Digital Imaging

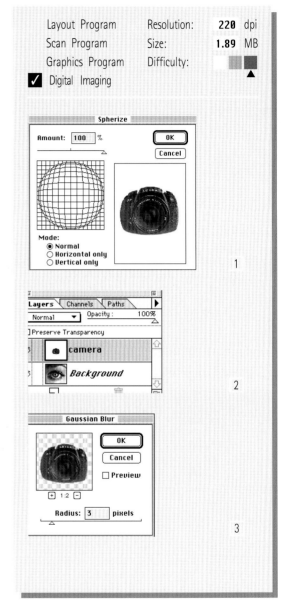

- Scan a black and white picture of a camera. Make the file the same size and resolution as the original halftone. Open the camera scan in Photoshop. (⌘O or **File**)

- Use the Marquee tool to select the center of the lens. *The M key toggles between the Rectangular and Elliptical marquee tools. Holding down the option key lets you start your selection from the center.*

- Apply the Spherize filter. (**Filter>Distort**) 1
        Amount: 100%   Mode: Normal

- Use the Magic Wand tool to select the camera. *To add to your selection, hold down the Shift. To subtract from your selection, hold down the Command key.*

- Open the original halftone in Photoshop. (⌘O or **File**)

- Duplicate the camera. (**Image**) Select the Move tool and drag the camera onto the original halftone.

- Open the Layers palette. (**Window>Palettes**) 2 Double-click on the layer "Floating Selection." *This opens the Make Layer dialog box.* Name the layer.

- Scale the camera image down to fit within the eye: Choose the Scale command. (**Image>Effects**) Click and drag one handle toward the center to shrink the image. *Hold the Shift key to constrain the image proportions.*

- Apply the Gaussian Blur filter. (**Filter>Blur**) 3
        Radius: 3 pixels

- Choose Add Layer Mask from the Layers palette pop-up menu. *The layer mask preview will appear.* Make Black the Foreground color. Use the Paintbrush tool to mask out desired areas of the camera.

- Choose Remove Layer Mask from the Layers palette pop-up menu.

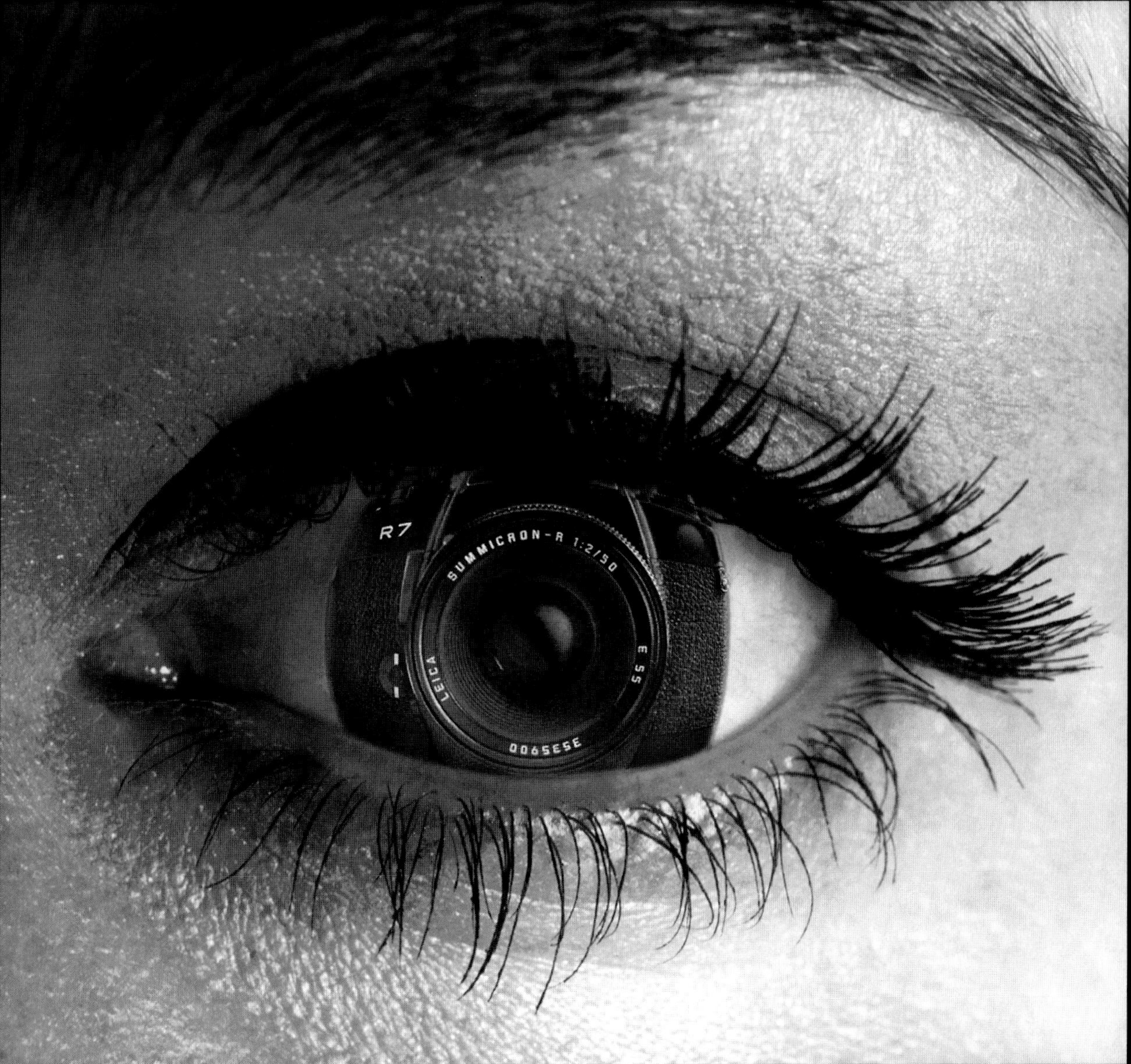
R7
SUMMICRON-R 1:2/50
LEICA
E 55

Masking

- Open the original halftone in Photoshop. (⌘O or **File**)

- Choose Add Layer Mask from the Layers palette pop-up menu.
  The layer mask preview will appear.
  Make Black the Foreground color.

- Double-click the Lasso tool. 1
    Feather: 10 pixels   Check Anti-aliased.
  Use the Lasso tool to create the trapezoidal section of the keyhole. *Holding the Option key draws straight lines.*

- Use the elliptical Marquee tool to create the circular section of the keyhole:
  Double-click on the Marquee tool. 2
    Shape: Elliptical
  Holding the Shift constrains the eclipse to a circle and adds to the previous selection. Holding the Option key allows the circle to originate from the center.

- Feather the selection. (**Select**)
    Radius: 30 pixels

- Inverse the selection. (**Select**)

- Make Black the Foreground color.
  Apply a Fill. (**Edit**) 3
    Use: Foreground Color
    Opacity: 100%
    Mode: Normal

- Choose Remove Layer Mask from the Layers palette pop-up menu.

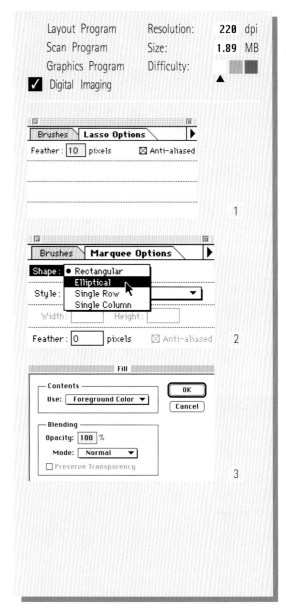

Layout Program Resolution: **220** dpi
Scan Program Size: **1.89** MB
Graphics Program Difficulty:
☑ Digital Imaging ▲

Brushes | Lasso Options ▶
Feather: 10 pixels ☒ Anti-aliased

1

Brushes | Marquee Options ▶
Shape: ● Rectangular
  Elliptical
Style: Single Row
  Single Column
Width: Height:
Feather: 0 pixels ☒ Anti-aliased

2

Fill
Contents
Use: Foreground Color ▼
OK
Cancel
Blending
Opacity: 100 %
Mode: Normal ▼
☐ Preserve Transparency

3

Partial Blur

- Open the file "Colorizing" from page 116 in Photoshop.
  (⌘O or **File**)

- Click on the Quick Mask mode.

- Make Black the Foreground color.

- Use the Paintbrush tool to mask desired areas of the image.
  A red overlay (akin to a rubylith) will appear.
  Toggle back to the Standard selection mode.
  *The Q key toggles between the Standard selection mode and
  the Quick Mask mode.*

- Apply the Gaussian Blur filter. (**Filter>Blur**)
      Radius: 15 pixels

- Open the Curves dialog box. (⌘**M** or **Image>Adjust**) 1
  Lighten the image by adjusting the curve accordingly.

- Increase the amount of Cyan in the image:
  Choose the Variations command. (**Image>Adjust**) 2
  Click on the More Cyan thumbnail image once.
  Click OK.

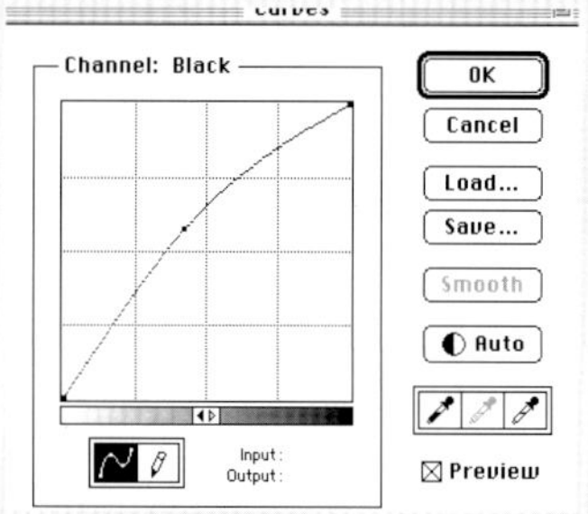

Layout Program	Resolution: **220** dpi
Scan Program	Size: **7.54** MB
Graphics Program	Difficulty:
✓ Digital Imaging	

1

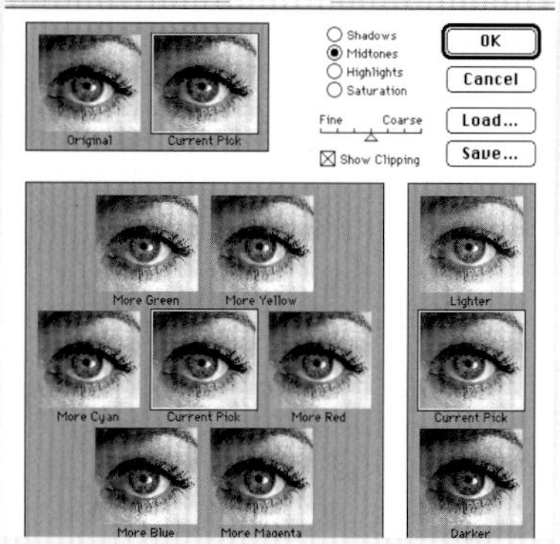

2

Collage

Layout Program	Resolution:	**220**	dpi
Scan Program	Size:	**7.54**	MB
Graphics Program	Difficulty:		
✓ Digital Imaging	▲		

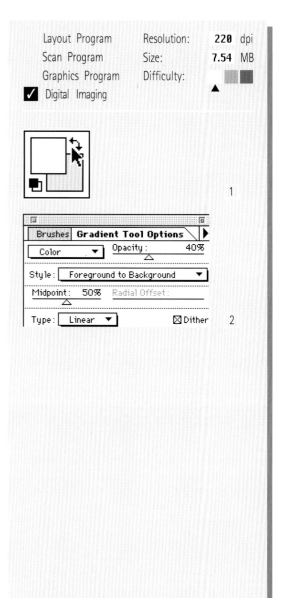

- Open the original halftone in Photoshop. (⌘**O** or **File**)

- Select the CMYK mode option. (**Mode**)

- Select a white Foreground and yellow Background color: Click on the respective color swatch and select the desired color within the Color Picker. 1

- Use the Marquee tool to select a rectangular stripe across the image. Offset it by clicking and dragging with the mouse.

- Switch the foreground and background colors.
  Double-click on the Gradient Tool. 2
  - Paint mode: Color   Opacity: 40%
  - Style: Foreground to Background
  - Midpoint skew: 50%
  - Type: Linear   Check Dither.
  Create a gradient by dragging from one side of the selection to the other.

- Create the remaining vertical and horizontal stripes in the same manner but use different colors for the gradients in conjunction with white.

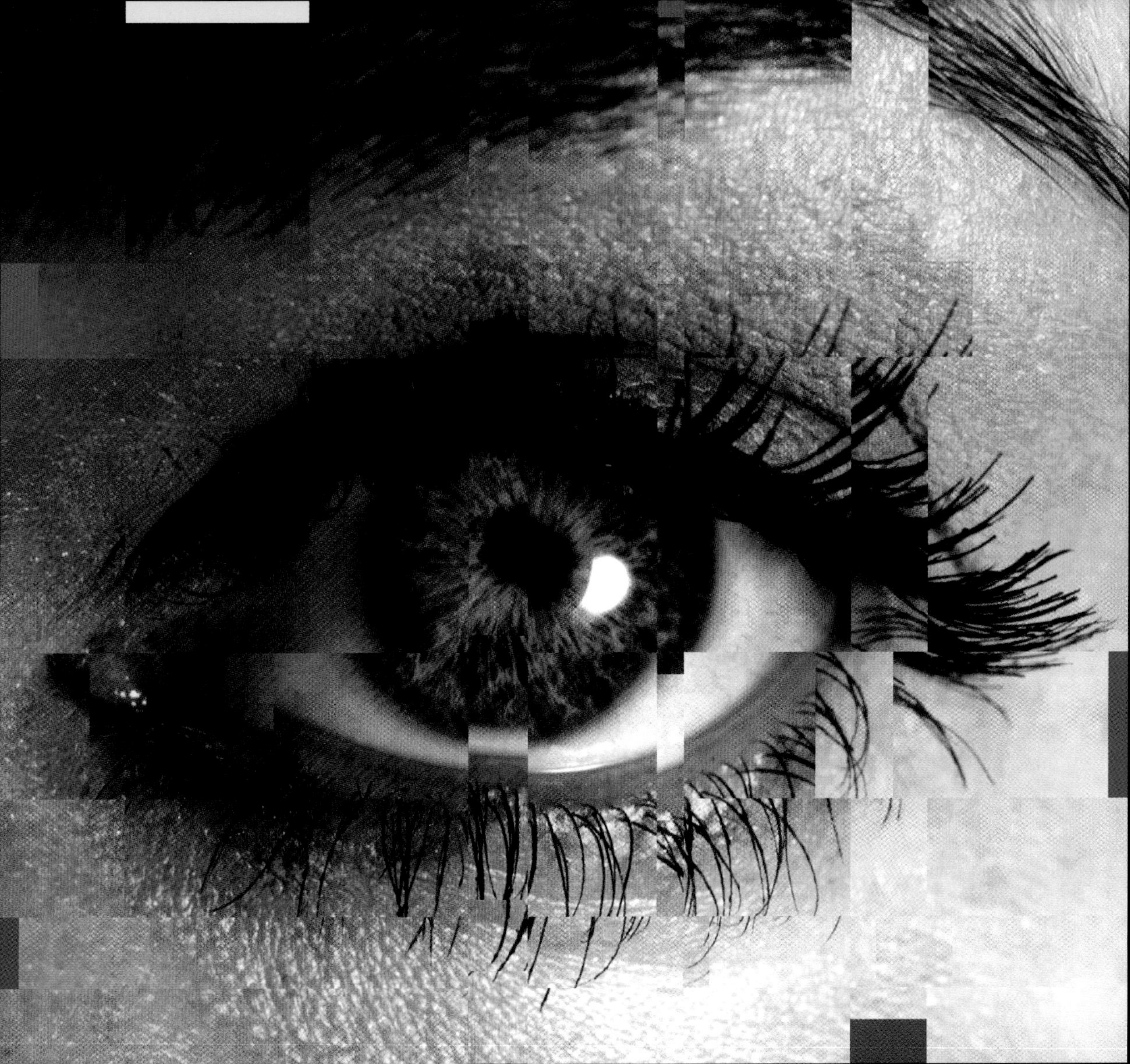

DRAWING TECHNIQUES

Practically every drawing and painting technique can be simulated on the computer. Various software filters play a large role in creating the illustrated presentation techniques. Completely unique drawing and painting techniques can create an image with impact.

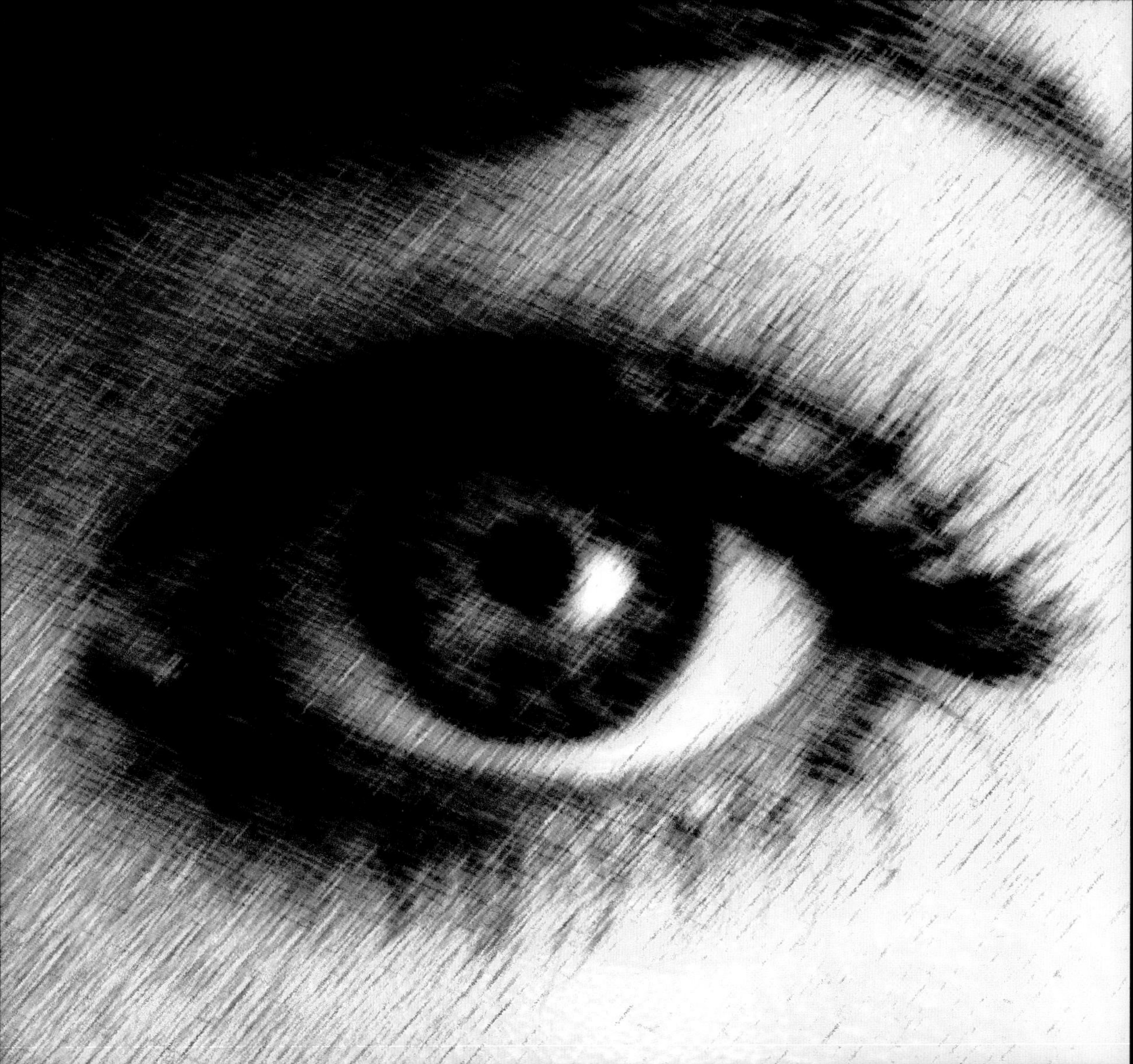

Shredding

- Open the original halftone in Photoshop. (⌘**O** or **File**)

- Open the Channels palette. (**Window>Palettes**)
  Create a New Channel.

- Apply the following filters in this order:
  Add Noise (**Filter>Noise**) 1
      Amount: 999   Distribution: Gaussian
  Motion Blur (**Filter>Blur**) 2
      Angle: 12°   Distance: 60 pixels
  Find Edges (**Filter>Stylize**)
  Gaussian Blur (**Filter>Blur**) 3
      Radius: 3 pixels

- Select All. (⌘**A** or **Select**)
  Choose the Define Pattern command. (**Edit**)

- Target the Black channel of the original image.
  Select the Bitmap mode option. (**Mode**) 4
      Output: 300 pixels/inch   Method: Custom Pattern

▶ *Page 155 (Chapter Title Page): Colored Pencil Texture*
Open the original halftone in Photoshop. (⌘O or File)
Select the RGB mode option. (Mode)
Open the Channels palette. (Window>Palettes)
Target the Red Channel. (⌘1) 5
Apply the following filters:
Pointillize (Filter>Pixelate) 6
   Cell Size: 7
Motion Blur (Filter>Blur)
   Angle: 12°   Distance: 60 pixels
Sharpen More (Filter>Sharpen)
Repeat the same filter sequence on the Green Channel.
Enter a different angle in the Motion Blur dialog box.
Target the whole image in the RGB Channel.
Apply the Diffuse filter. (Filter>Stylize)
   Mode: Normal

Layout Program	Resolution:	**300** dpi
Scan Program	Size:	**0.45** MB
Graphics Program	Difficulty:	
✓ Digital Imaging		▲

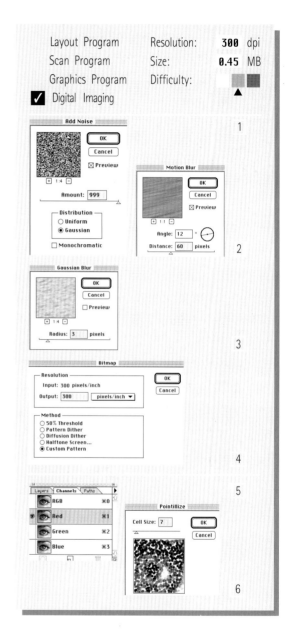

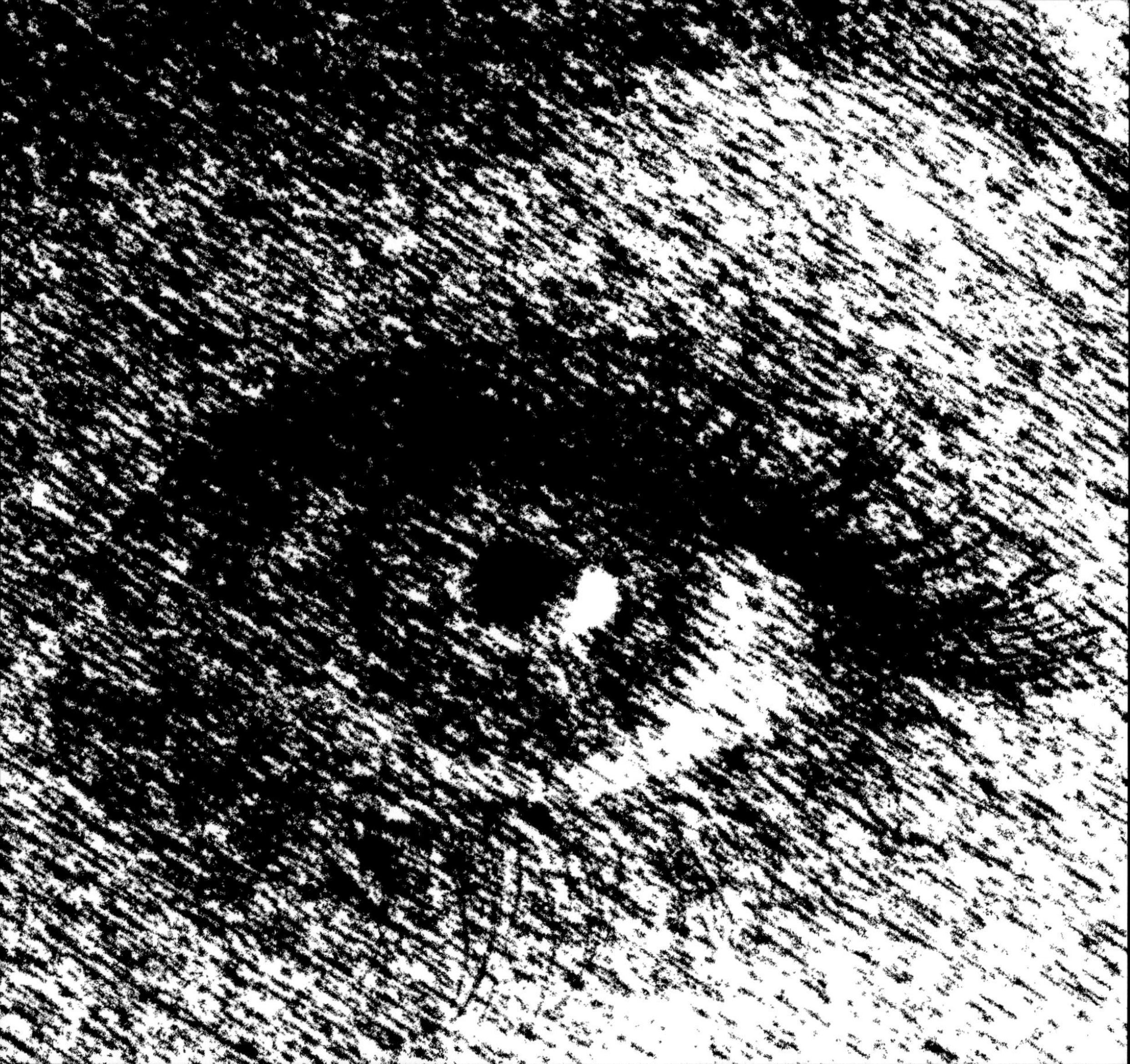

Wood Carving

- Open the original halftone in Photoshop. (**⌘O** or **File**)
- Apply the Gaussian Blur filter. (**Filter>Blur**) 1
    Radius: 3 pixels
- Apply the Find Edges filter. (**Filter>Stylize**)
- Open the Brightness/Contrast dialog box.
  (**⌘B** or **Image>Adjust**) 2
    Brightness: -22
    Contrast: 100
- Select the Bitmap mode option. (**Mode**) 3
    Output: 300 pixels/inch
    Method: 50% Threshold

Layout Program | Resolution: | **300** dpi
Scan Program | Size: | **0.45** MB
Graphics Program | Difficulty:
✓ Digital Imaging

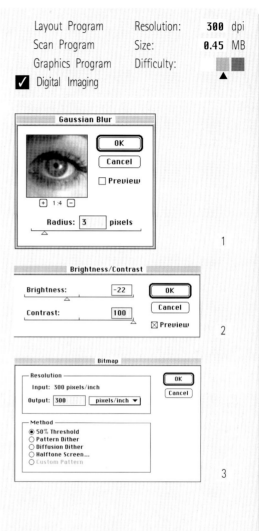

Photocopied Effect

- Open the original halftone in Photoshop. (**⌘O** or **File**)
- Apply the High Pass filter. (**Filter>Other**) 1
    Radius: 100 pixels
- Apply the Sharpen More filter. (**Filter>Sharpen**)
- Select the Bitmap mode option. (**Mode**) 2
    Output: 300 pixels/inch
    Method: 50% Threshold

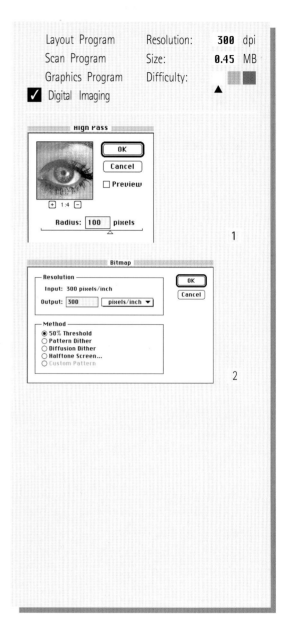

Layout Program   Resolution: **300** dpi
Scan Program   Size: **0.45** MB
Graphics Program   Difficulty:
☑ Digital Imaging

Pastels

- Open the original halftone in Photoshop. (⌘O or **File**)

- Open the Brightness/Contrast dialog box.
  (⌘B or **Image>Adjust**) 1
    Brightness: 50   Contrast: 95

- Apply the Color Range command to select all of the black
  in the image. (**Select**) 2
  With the Eyedropper tool, click on a black area in the
  preview window or in the image.
    Select: Sampled Colors
    Fuzziness: 40
    Check Image.

- Use Save Selection to save selected areas to a new Channel.
  (**Select**)

- Select the RGB mode option. (**Mode**)

- Click on the foreground color swatch and select a color
  within the Color Picker. *A shade of brown was used for the
  example.*

- Select All. (⌘A or **Select**)
  Apply a Fill. (**Edit**) 3
    Use: Foreground Color
    Opacity: 100%
    Mode: Normal

- Double-click on the Paintbrush tool. 4
    Paint Mode: Dissolve
    Opacity: 70%
  Use various brush intensities, foreground colors, paint tools
  (i.e. airbrush or pencil) and opacity settings to create a
  chalk pastel effect over the image.

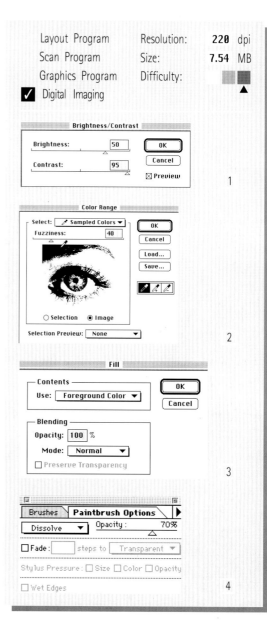

Layout Program
Scan Program
Graphics Program
✓ Digital Imaging

Resolution: **220** dpi
Size: **7.54** MB
Difficulty:

Brightness/Contrast
Brightness: 50
Contrast: 95
OK
Cancel
☒ Preview

1

Color Range
Select: ✎ Sampled Colors ▾
Fuzziness: 40
OK
Cancel
Load...
Save...
○ Selection ● Image
Selection Preview: None ▾

2

Fill
Contents
Use: Foreground Color ▾
OK
Cancel
Blending
Opacity: 100 %
Mode: Normal ▾
☐ Preserve Transparency

3

Brushes | Paintbrush Options
Dissolve ▾ Opacity: 70%
☐ Fade: ___ steps to Transparent ▾
Stylus Pressure: ☐ Size ☐ Color ☐ Opacity
☐ Wet Edges

4

Sepia

- Create an RGB scan of a coarse piece of watercolor paper. Make the file the same size and resolution as the original halftone. Open the scan in Photoshop. (⌘O or **File**)

- Open the original halftone in Photoshop. (⌘O or **File**) Select the RGB mode option. (**Mode**) Select All (⌘A or **Select**) and Copy (⌘C or **Edit**) the image.

- Target the watercolor paper image. Open the Channels palette. (**Window>Palettes**) Create a new Channel. Paste the copied image into the Channel. (⌘V or **Edit**)

- Open the Brightness/Contrast dialog box. (⌘B or **Image>Adjust**) 1
  Brightness: 50   Contrast: 95

- Apply the Minimum filter. (**Filter>Other**) 2
  Radius: 6 pixels
  Apply the Gaussian Blur filter. (**Filter>Blur**) 3
  Radius: 6 pixels

- Open the Levels dialog box. (⌘L or **Image>Adjust**) 4
  Input Levels: Black: 36   Gamma: 1.00   White: 45

- Invert the image. (⌘I or **Image>Adjust**)

- Open the Channels palette. (**Window>Palettes**) Target the RGB Channel. Use the Load Selection command to load the saved selection. (**Select**)

- Open the Levels dialog box. (⌘L or **Image>Adjust**) 5
  Input Levels: Black: 176   Gamma: 1.00   White: 255

- Tint the image with brown, orange and violet tones:
  Double-click the Airbrush tool. 6
      Paint mode: Color   Opacity: 14%
  Select an appropriate brush size.
  Define a Foreground color for each pass.

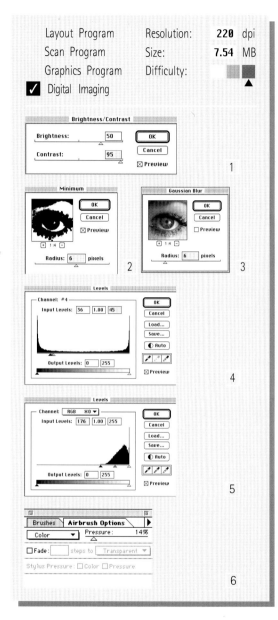

Layout Program   Resolution: **220** dpi
Scan Program   Size: **7.54** MB
Graphics Program   Difficulty:
☑ Digital Imaging

Stipple Technique

- Open the original halftone in Photoshop. (**⌘O** or **File**)

- Open the Image Size dialog box. (**Image**) 1
      Constrain: Proportions
      Resolution: 50 pixels/inch

- Apply the Gaussian Blur filter. (**Filter>Blur**) 2
      Radius: 2 pixels

- Open the Posterize dialog box. (**Image>Map**)
      Levels: 5

- Apply the Diffuse filter four times. (**Filter>Stylize**) 3
      Mode: Normal
   Shortcut: ⌘F reapplies the last filter.

- Apply the Add Noise filter. (**Filter>Distort**) 4
      Radius: 2 pixels   Distribution: Gaussian

- Open the Image Size dialog box. (**Image**)
      Constrain: Proportions
      Resolution: 220 pixels/inch

- Apply the Diffuse filter five times. (**Filter>Stylize**) 3
      Mode: Normal
   Shortcut: ⌘F reapplies the last filter.

- Open the Posterize dialog box. (**Image>Map**)
      Levels: 5

- Select the RGB mode. (**Mode**)
   Select the Indexed Colors mode. (**Mode**)

- Open the Color Table dialog box. (**Mode**) 5
      Table: Grayscale
   Select a group of squares (values) from two of the tonal
   values. Choose colors from the Color Picker.

- Repeat the procedure for all remaining gray levels.

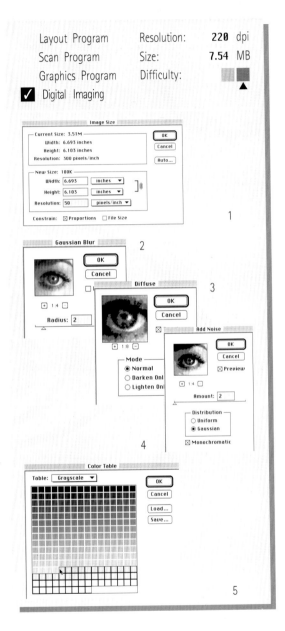

Layout Program	Resolution:	**220** dpi
Scan Program	Size:	**7.54** MB
Graphics Program	Difficulty:	
✓ Digital Imaging		

1

2

3

4

5

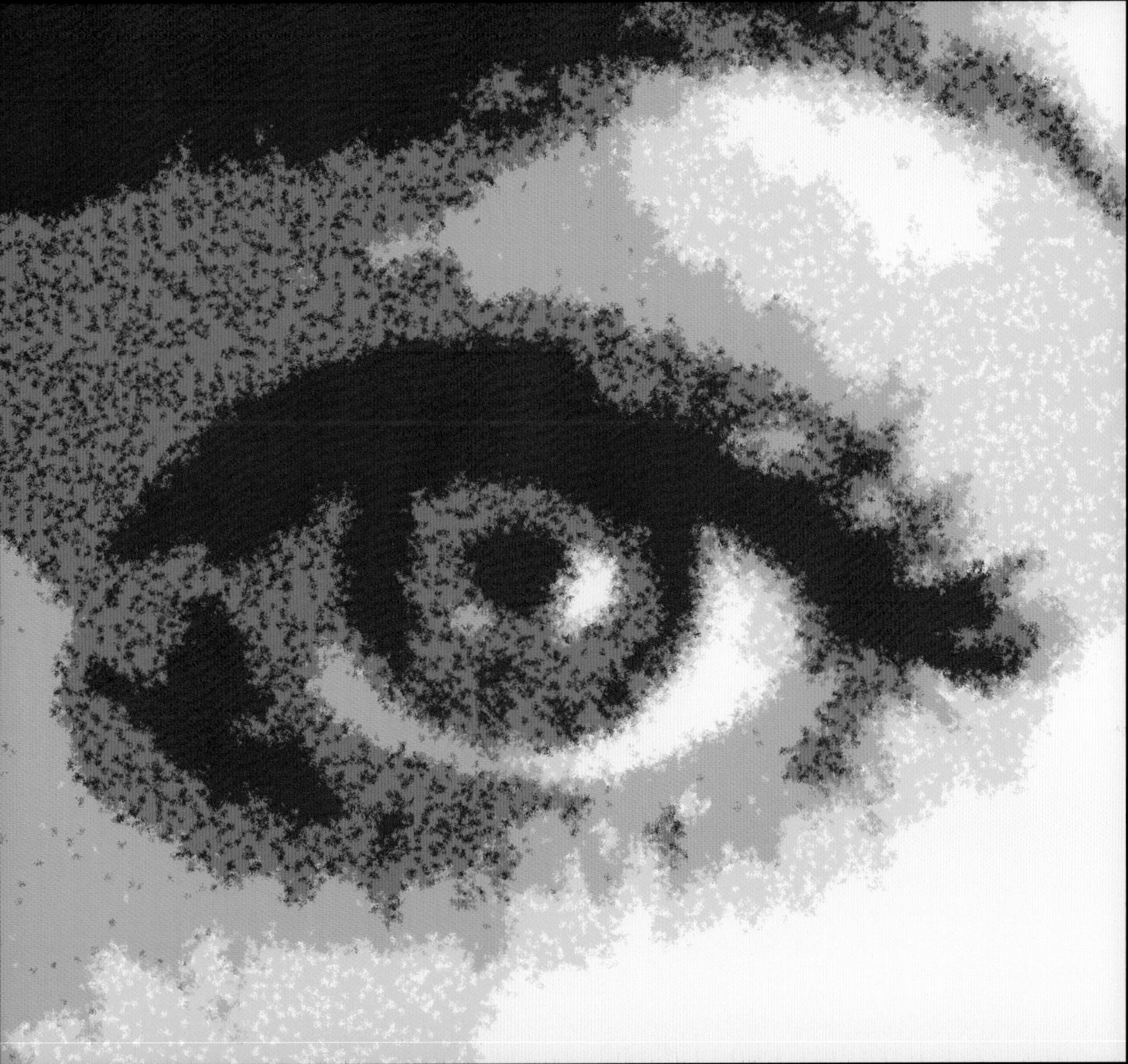

Color Foils

- Open the original halftone in Photoshop. (**⌘O** or **File**)

- Apply the Gaussian Blur filter. (**Filter>Blur**) 1
  Radius: 6 pixels
  Open the Posterize dialog box. (**Image>Map**) 2
  Levels: 7

- Select the RGB mode. (**Mode**)
  Select the Indexed Colors mode. (**Mode**)

- Open the Color Table dialog box. (**Mode**) 3
  Table: Grayscale
  Select a group of squares (values) from two of the tonal values. Choose colors from the Color Picker.

- Repeat the procedure for all remaining gray levels.

▶ *Page 172: Watercolor*
  *Open the original halftone in Photoshop. (**⌘O** or **File**)*
  Apply the Watercolor filter from Aldus Gallery Effects
  (supplied with Photoshop™ 3.0.) 4
  *Select the RGB mode. (**Mode**)*
  *Select the Indexed Colors mode. (**Mode**)*
  *Colorize the image using the Color Table. (**Mode**) 3*

▶ *Page 173: Oil*
  *Open the original halftone in Photoshop. (**⌘O** or **File**)*
  Double-Click on the Rubber Stamp tool. 5
  *   Painting mode: Dissolve   Option: Impressionist mode*
  Hold down the Option key and click for a source point.
  Click and drag to paint with the sampled image.
  Arbitrarily manipulate the image using various tools,
  opacities and brushes. The Smudge and Blur tools are
  recommended to duplicate the example.
  *Select the RGB mode. (**Mode**)*
  *Select the Indexed Colors mode. (**Mode**)*
  *Colorize the image using the Color Table. (**Mode**) •3*
  Rework the color transitions with the Rubber Stamp tool.

3

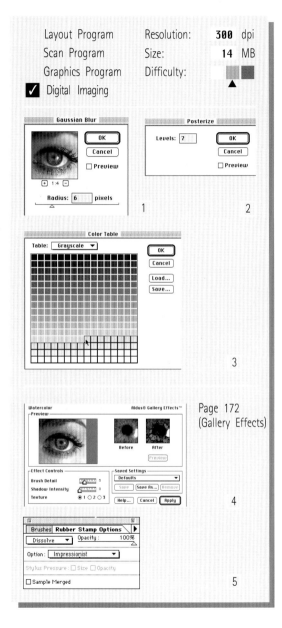

Layout Program
Scan Program
Graphics Program
☑ Digital Imaging

Resolution: **300** dpi
Size: 14 MB
Difficulty:

1

2

3

Page 172
(Gallery Effects)

4

5

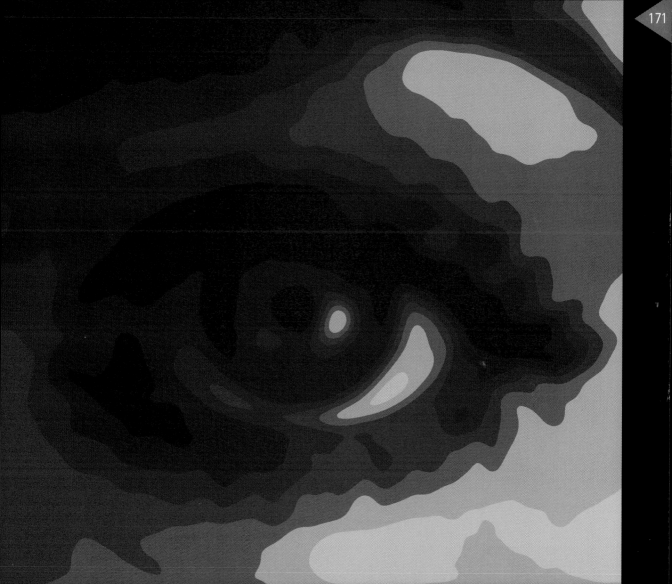

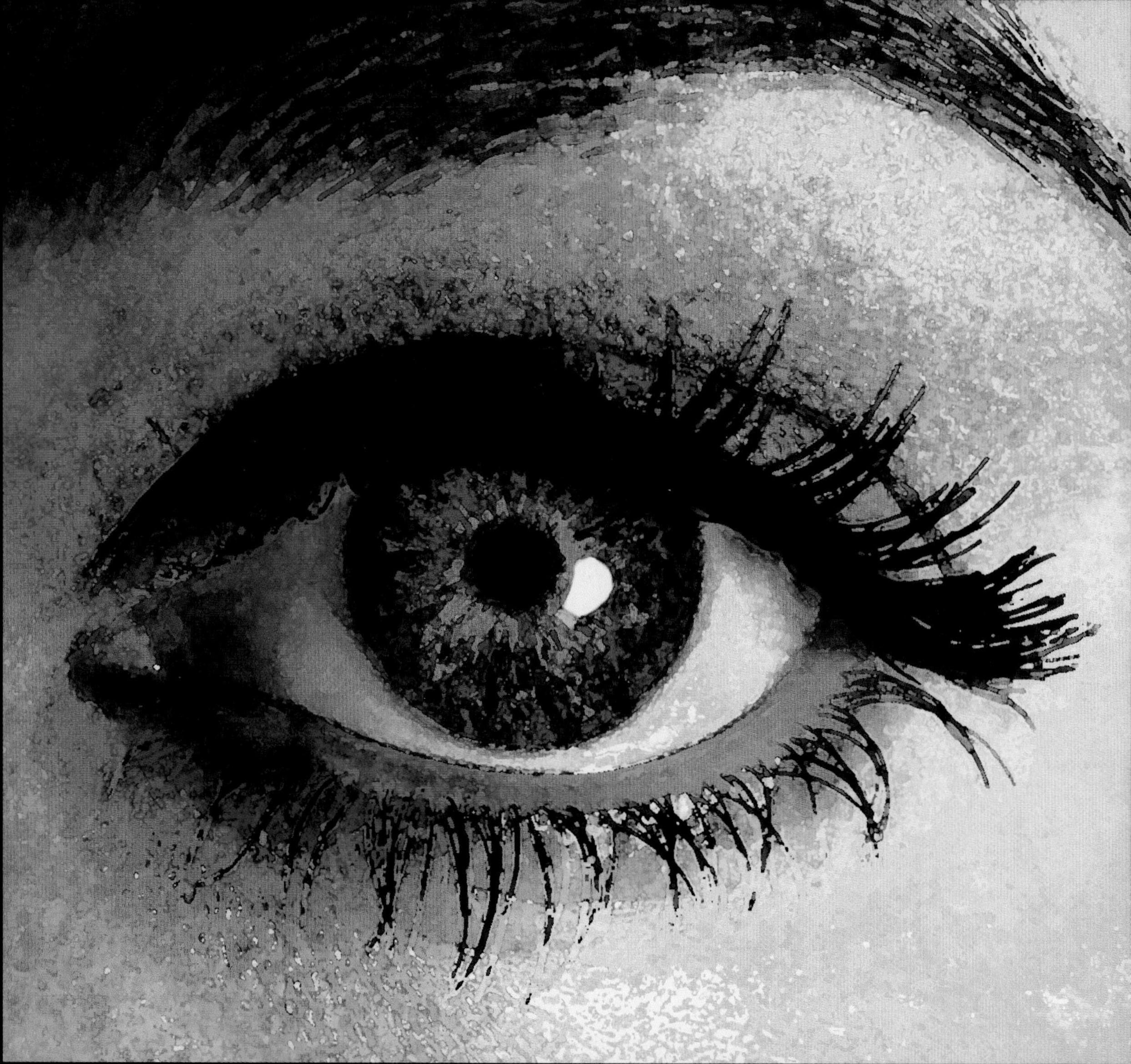

Airbrush

- Open the original halftone in Photoshop. (⌘O or **File**)

- Open the Brightness/Contrast dialog box.
  (⌘B or **Image>Adjust**) 1
    Brightness: 25   Contrast: 100

- Select All (⌘A or **Select**) and Cut (⌘X or **Edit**) the image.

- Open the Channels palette. (**Window>Palettes**) 2
  Create a new Channel.
  Paste the copied image into the channel. (⌘V or **Edit**)

- Invert the image. (⌘I or **Image>Map**)

- Target the Black channel.
  Set the Foreground and Background default colors.

- Double-click on the Gradient Tool in the Toolbox. 3
    Paint Mode: Color   Opacity: 100%
    Style: Foreground to Background
    Midpoint Skew: 50%
    Type: Linear   Check Dither.
  Start at the bottom of the image and drag to the top.

- Use the Load Selection command to load the saved
  selection. (**Select**) 4

- Use the None command to deselect the selection.
  (⌘D or **Select**)

- Select the CMYK mode option. (**Mode**)

- Open the Hue/Saturation dialog box.
  (⌘U or **Image>Adjust**)
  Select Colorize and use the sliders to adjust the image.
      Hue: -146   Saturation: 55   Lightness: 0

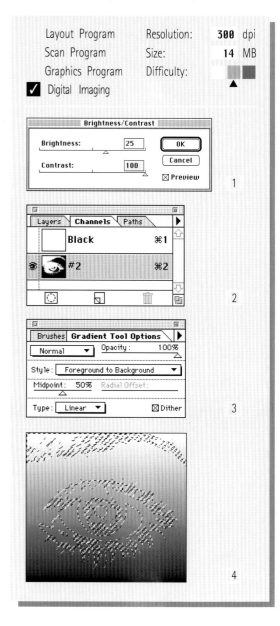

Layout Program   Resolution: **300** dpi
Scan Program   Size: 14 MB
Graphics Program   Difficulty:
✓ Digital Imaging

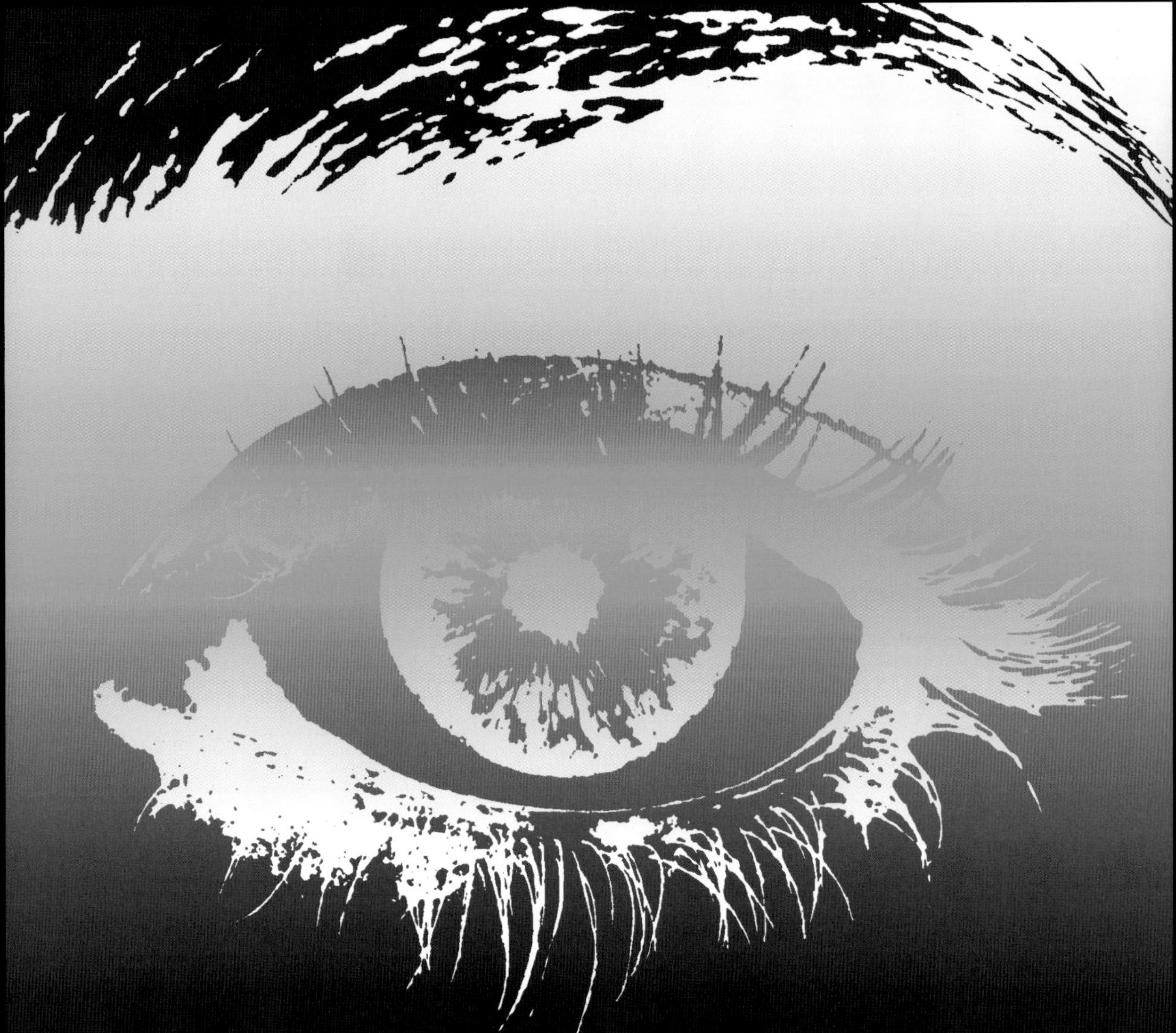

Silk-Screened Effect

- Trace a rough outline of the original image on a sheet of tracing paper. Scan the tracing in black and white. Make the file the same size and resolution as the original halftone. Open the scan in Photoshop. (⌘O or **File**) Select All (⌘A or **Select**) and Copy (⌘C or **Edit**) the image.

- Open the original halftone in Photoshop. (⌘O or **File**) Select the RGB mode option. (**Mode**) Open the Layers palette. (**Window>Palettes**) Create a new Layer. Name it "Outline." Paste the copied image into the layer. (⌘U or **Edit**)

- Use Color Range to select all the white in the image. (**Select**) 1 With the Eyedropper tool, click on any white area in the preview window or in the image.
  Select: Sampled Colors   Fuzziness: 10   Check Image. Delete the selection. *This will rid the scan of its white background, leaving it transparent.*

- Target the Background layer.
  Open the Brightness/Contrast dialog box. 2
  (⌘B or **Image>Adjust**)   Brightness: 0   Contrast: 95
  Open the Hue/Saturation dialog box. (⌘U or **Image>Adjust**)
  Select Colorize. Hue: -122   Saturation: 32   Lightness: -24

- Target the "Outline" layer. Check Preserve Transparency.
  Pick a red Foreground color. Pick a yellow Background color.
  Double-click on the Gradient Tool. 3
        Paint mode: Normal   Opacity: 100%.
        Style: Foreground to Background
        Midpoint skew: 50%
        Type: Linear   Check Dither.
  Drag the gradient tool diagonally across the image.

- Use the Move tool to offset the "Outline" layer.

- Create a new layer. Name it "Layer 1." Pick a new Foreground color. Use the Lasso tool to select two areas. Fill the selections. (**Edit**)

- Change the order of the Layers: Select the "Layer 1" on the Layers palette. Drag it underneath the "Outline" layer. 4

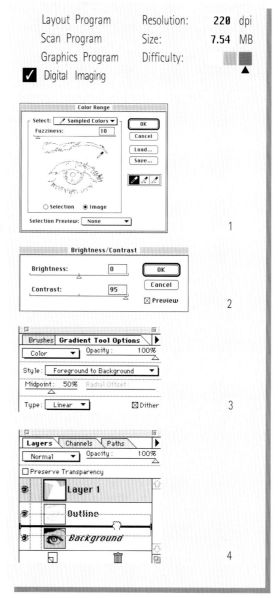

Layout Program	Resolution:	**220** dpi
Scan Program	Size:	**7.54** MB
Graphics Program	Difficulty:	
✓ Digital Imaging		▲

1

2

3

4

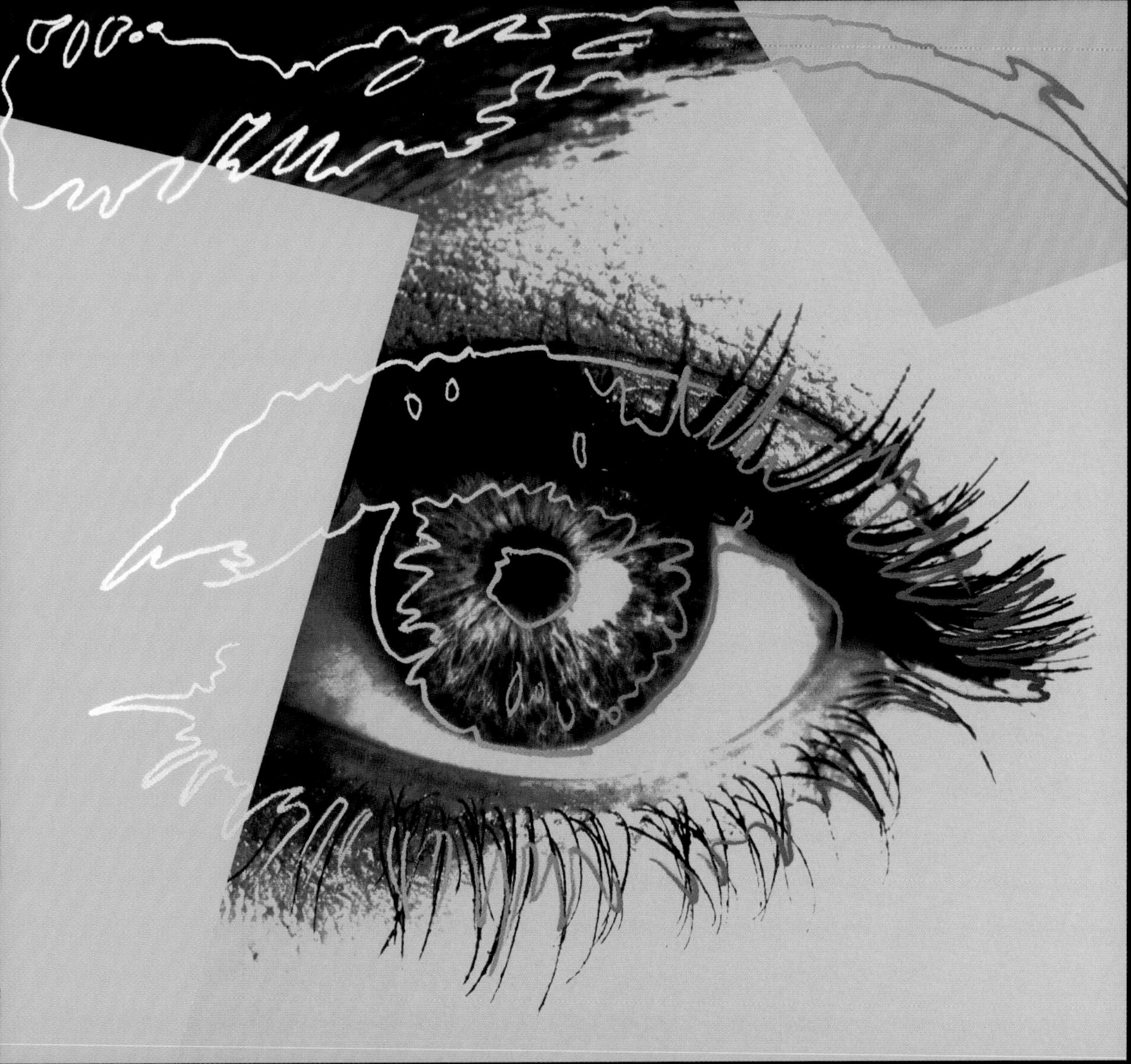

ILLUSTRATIONS

The boundary between photography and illustration is becoming more and more subtle. Illustrative options are also boundless using digital image manipulation. To create these examples, the degree of abstraction was restricted to maintain size and likeness of the original photographic image.

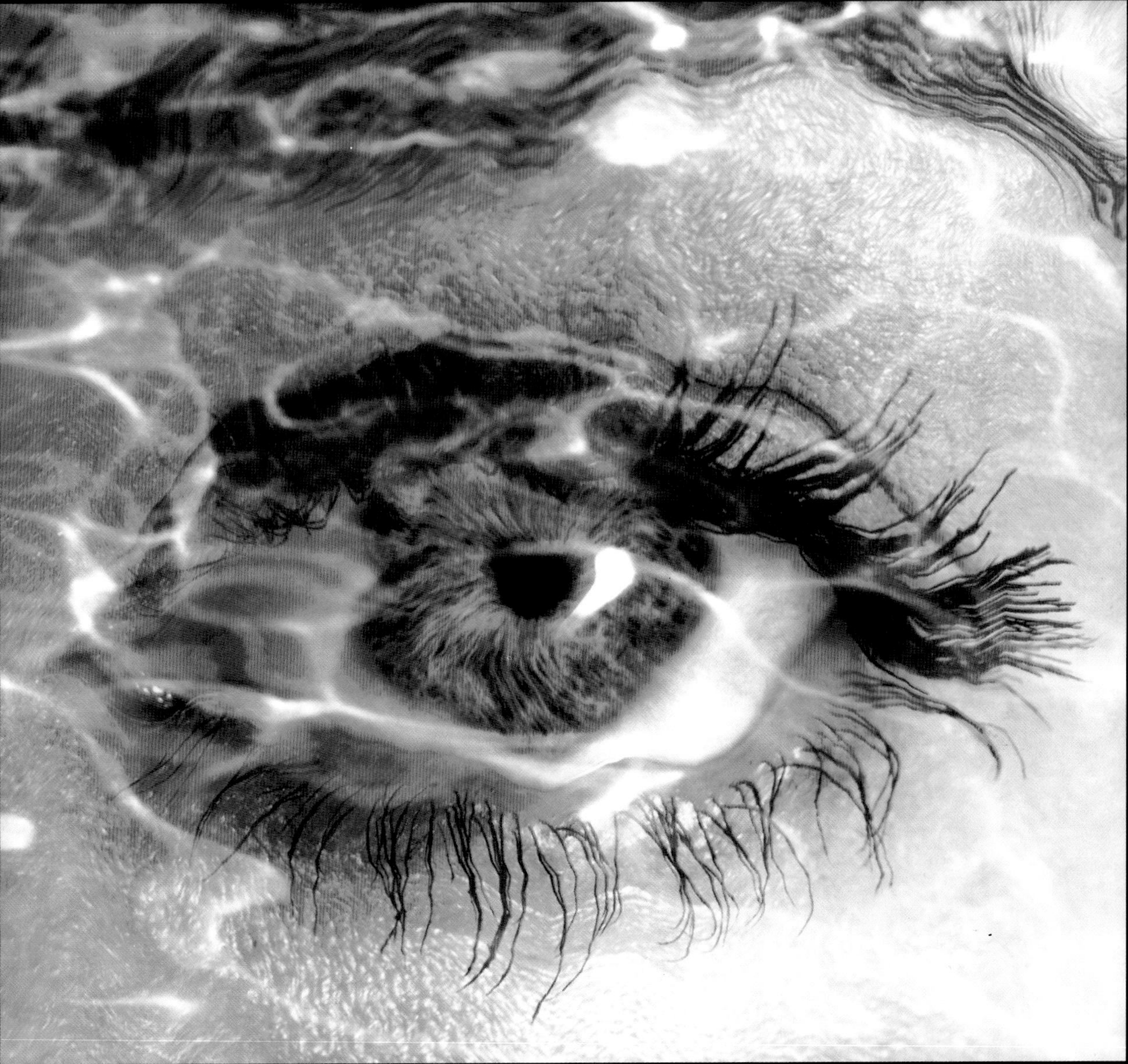

Patchwork

- Open the original halftone in Photoshop. (⌘O or **File**)

- Use the rectangular Marquee tool to select several sections of the image. Open the Levels dialog box. (⌘L or **Image>Adjust**) Apply distinctive modifications to the brightness, contrast and tonal range in each selection.

- Select the CMYK mode option. (**Mode**)

- Use the rectangular Marquee tool to select another section. Open the Hue/Saturation dialog box. (⌘U or **Image>Adjust**) 1 Select Colorize and use the sliders to adjust the image.

  Hue: -7   Saturation: 88   Lightness: -7

- Inverse the selection. (**Select**)
  Open the Hue/Saturation dialog box. (⌘U or **Image>Adjust**) 2
  Select Colorize.   Hue: 180   Saturation: 30   Lightness: 0

▶ *Page 179 (Chapter Title Page): Reflection in Water*
Scan an image of reflecting water in black and white.
Make the file the same size and resolution as the original
*halftone. Open the scan in Photoshop. (⌘O or **File**)*
*Open the original halftone in Photoshop. (⌘O or **File**)*
*Apply the Wave filter. (**Filter>Distort**) 3*
  Number of Generations: 4
  Wavelength: Minimum 1, Maximum 330
  Amplitude: Minimum 1, Maximum 55
  Scale: Horizontal: 100%, Vertical: 100%
  Type: Triangle   Undefined Areas: Repeat Edge Pixels
*Select All (⌘A or **Select**) and Copy (⌘C or **Edit**) the image.*
Target the water image. Open the Layers palette.
*(**Window>Palette**) Create a new Layer. Name it "Original."*
*Paste the image in the Clipboard to the layer. (⌘U or **Edit**)*
Combine the two images. Set layer mode to Overlay. 4
*Open the original halftone in Photoshop. (⌘O or **File**)*
*Select the CMYK mode option. (**Mode**)*
*Open the Hue/Saturation dialog box. (⌘U or **Image>Adjust**)*
Select Colorize.   Hue: -173   Saturation: 100 Lightness: 0

Layout Program	Resolution:	**220** dpi
Scan Program	Size:	**7.54** MB
Graphics Program	Difficulty:	
✓ Digital Imaging		▲

1

2

Page 179

3

4

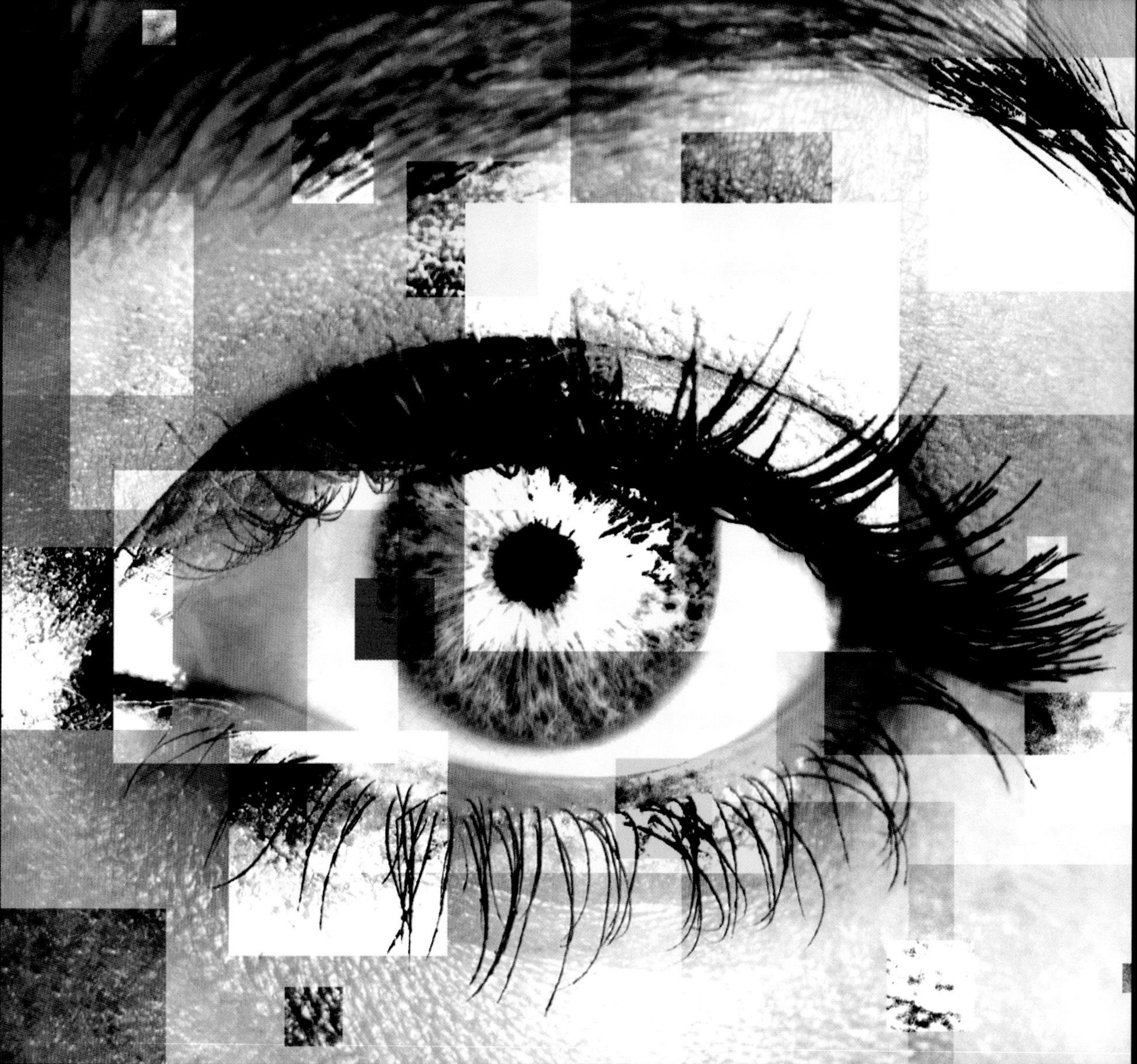

Checkboard Pattern

Layout Program   Resolution: **220** dpi
Scan Program   Size: **7.54** MB
Graphics Program   Difficulty:
✓ Digital Imaging

- Within FreeHand, construct a checkerboard pattern the same size as the original image.
  Export the illustration as an EPS file. (**⌘E** or **File**)

- Open the exported EPS file into Photoshop. (**⌘O** or **File**)

- Apply the Spherize filter. (**Filter>Distort**) 1
       Amount: 100%   Mode: Normal

- Select All (**⌘A** or **Select**) and Copy (**⌘C** or **Edit**) the image.

- Open the original halftone in Photoshop. (**⌘O** or **File**)

- Open the Channels palette. (**Window>Palettes**)
  Create a new Channel. Name it "Checkerboard."
  Paste the selection from the Clipboard. (**⌘V** or **Edit**)
  Return to the Black channel.

- Select the CMYK mode option. (**Mode**)

- Use Load Selection to load the saved selection "Checkerboard." (**Select**)

- Open the Hue/Saturation dialog box. (**⌘U** or **Image>Adjust**) 2
  Select Colorize and use the sliders to adjust the image.
       Hue: -169   Saturation: 78   Lightness: -30

- Inverse the selection. (**Select**)

- Open the Hue/Saturation dialog box. (**⌘U** or **Image>Adjust**) 3
  Select Colorize and use the sliders to adjust the image.
       Hue: -20   Saturation: 85   Lightness: -30

1

2

3

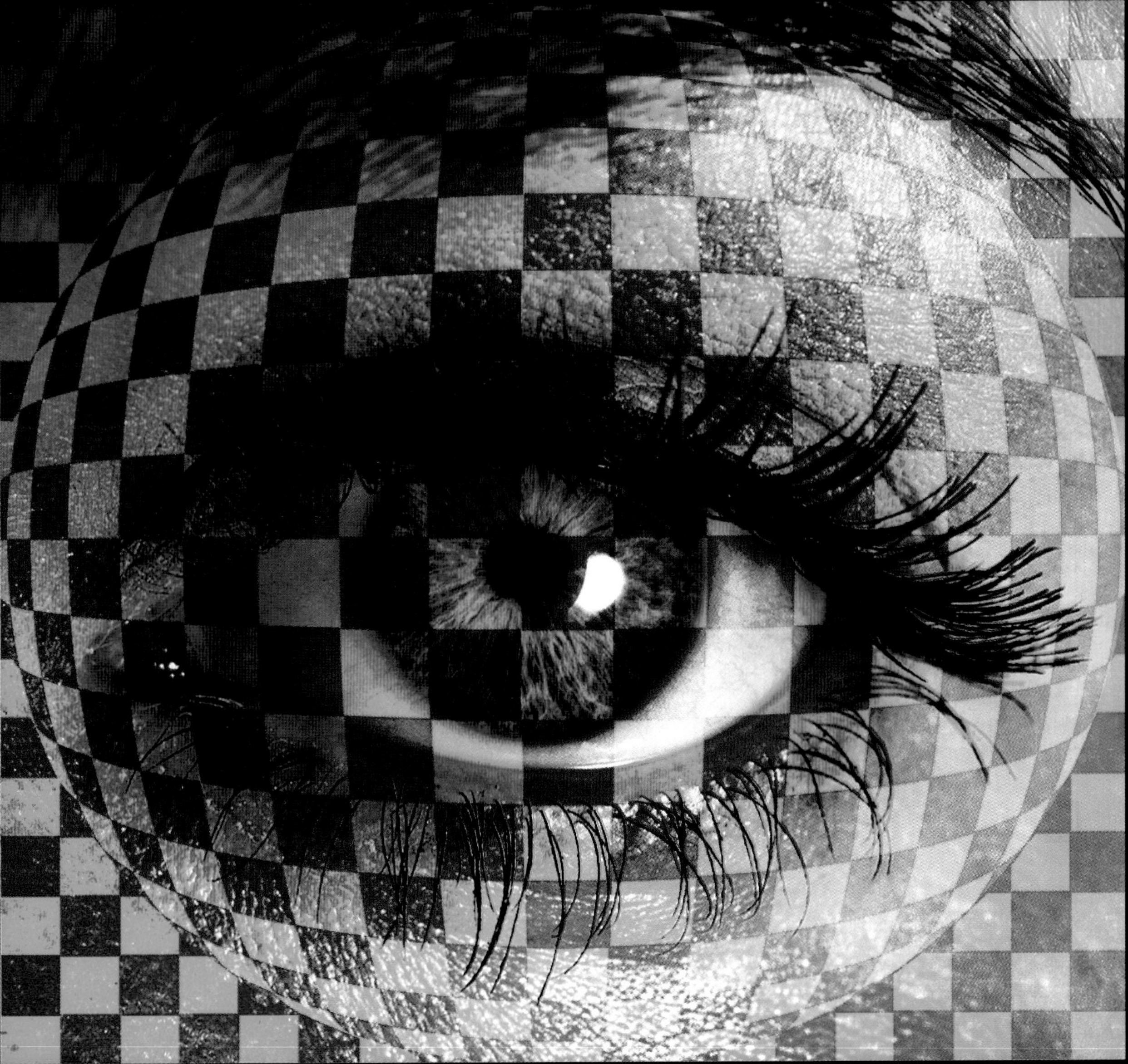

Foliage

- Scan an image of foliage in black and white. Make sure this file is the same size and resolution as the original halftone.

- Open the scan in Photoshop. (⌘O or **File**)

- Open the original halftone in Photoshop. (⌘O or **File**)

- Select the scanned foliage document.

- Open the Layers palette. (**Window>Palettes**)
Drag the layer from the Layers palette into the original halftone window.

- Double-click on that layer thumbnail to open the Layers Options dialog box. Name the layer "Foliage."
Adjust the Composite Controls. 1

- Choose Add Layer Mask from the layers palette pop-up menu. 2 The layer mask preview will appear.

- Use the Lasso tool to select an area. (In our case, the eyeball.)
Feather the selection. (**Select**) 3
    Radius: 30 pixels

- Apply a Fill. (**Edit**) 4
Shortcut: Shift & Delete brings up the Fill dialog box.
    Use: Black   Opacity: 100%   Mode: Normal

- Apply the mask permanently:
Choose Remove Layer Mask from layers palette pop-up menu. Click Apply.

- Select the CMYK mode option. (**Mode**)
Open the Hue/Saturation dialog box. 5
(**⌘U** or **Image>Adjust**)
Select Colorize and use the sliders to adjust the image.
    Hue: 60   Saturation: 50   Lightness: 0

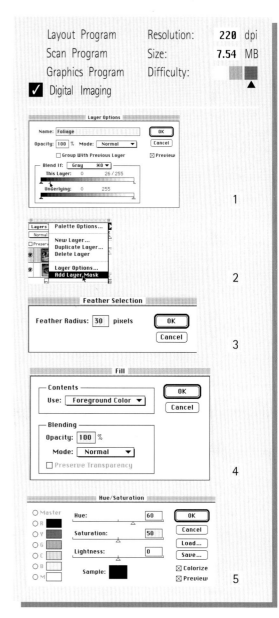

Combining Subjects

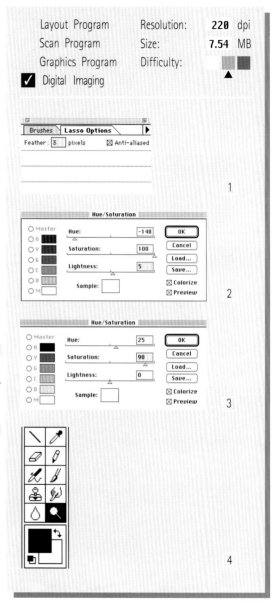

Layout Program   Resolution: **220** dpi
Scan Program   Size: **7.54** MB
Graphics Program   Difficulty:
✓ Digital Imaging

- Scan an image of water in black and white. Make sure this file is the same size and resolution as the original halftone.

- Open the scan in Photoshop. (⌘O or **File**)
Select All (⌘A or **Select**) and Copy (⌘C or **Edit**) the image.

- Open the original halftone in Photoshop. (⌘O or **File**)

- Select an area to paste into. (The eyeball, in our example.)
Double-click the Lasso tool.   1
       Feather: 3 pixels   Check Anti-aliased.

- Save the Selection. (**Select**)

- Apply the Paste Into command. (**Edit**)

- Select the CMYK mode option. (**Mode**)

- Use Load Selection to load the saved selection. (**Select**)

- Open the Hue/Saturation dialog box. (⌘U or **Image>Adjust**) 2
Select Colorize and use the sliders to adjust the image.
       Hue: -148   Saturation: 100   Lightness: 5

- Inverse the selection. (**Select**)

- Open the Hue/Saturation dialog box. (⌘U or **Image>Adjust**) 3
Select Colorize and use the sliders to adjust the image.
       Hue: 25   Saturation: 90   Lightness: 0

- Inverse the selection. (**Select**)

- Utilize the Dodge and Burn tools to strengthen the water effect.   4
Double-click on the Dodge (default) tool to toggle between the tools within the Toning Tools Options palette.
Shortcut: the O key toggles between all three Toning tools: Dodge, Burn, and Sponge.

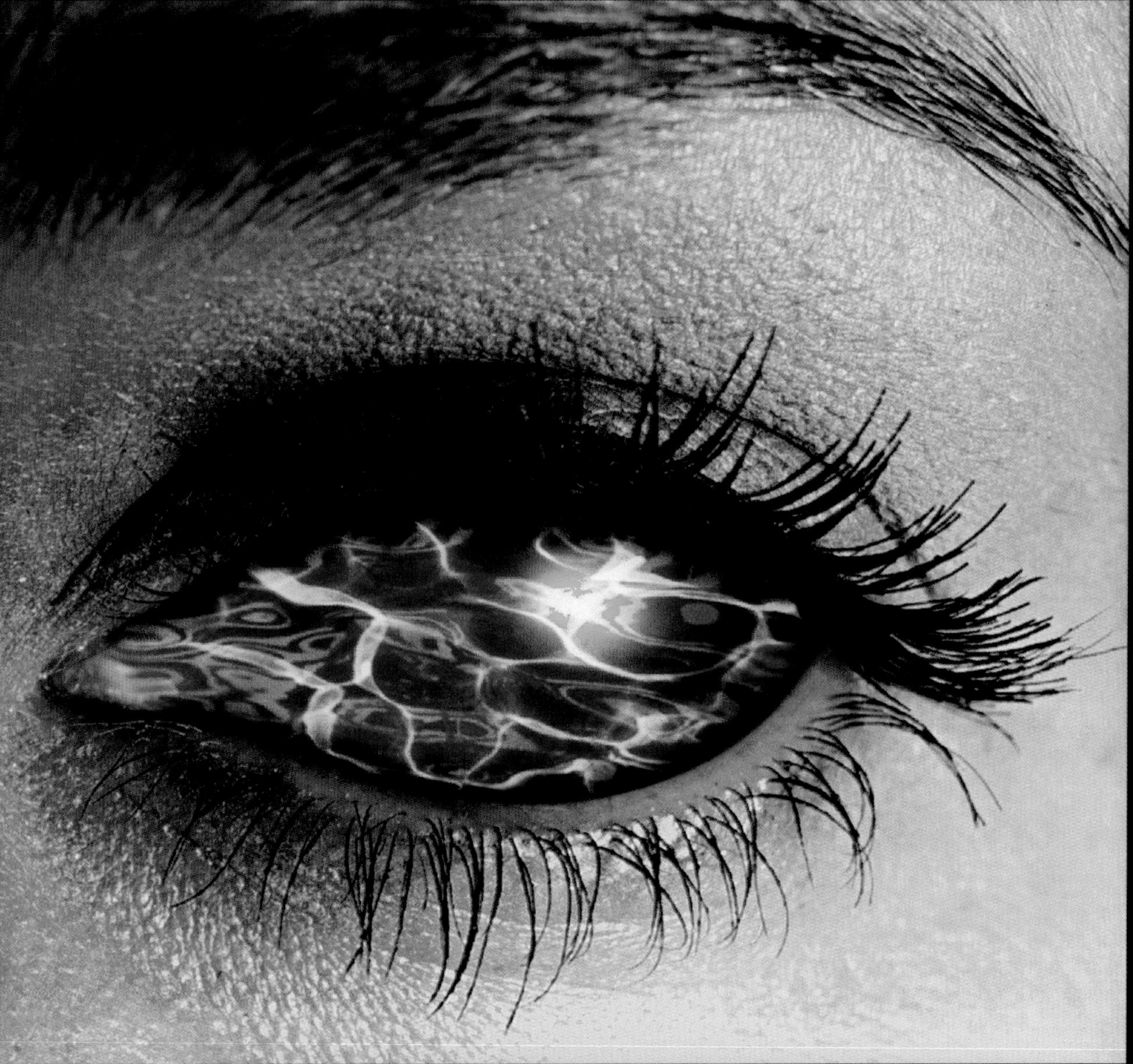

Gelatin Effect

Layout Program   Resolution: **220** dpi

Scan Program   Size: **7.54** MB

Graphics Program   Difficulty:

✓ Digital Imaging

- Open the original halftone in Photoshop. (⌘O or **File**)
  Open the Brightness/Contrast dialog box. 1
  (⌘B or **Image>Adjust**)   Brightness: 65   Contrast: 100
  Apply the Gaussian Blur filter. (**Filter>Blur**)   Radius: 20 pixels 2

- Open the Brightness/Contrast dialog box.
  (⌘B or **Image>Adjust**)   Brightness: 40   Contrast: 90
  Invert the image. (⌘I or **Image>Map**)
  Duplicate the image. (**Image**) Name the duplicate "Image 1." 3

- Apply the Offset filter. (**Filter>Other**)
       Horizontal: 12   Vertical: 8
       Undefined Areas: Repeat Edge Pixels
  Apply the Gaussian Blur filter. (**Filter>Blur**)   Radius: 8 pixels

- Open the Brightness/Contrast dialog box.
  (⌘B or **Image>Adjust**)   Brightness: 0   Contrast: -50

- Save changes to "Image 1." (⌘S or **File**)
  Duplicate "Image 1." (**Image**) Name the duplicate "Image 2."

- Apply the Offset filter. (**Filter>Other**) 4
       Horizontal: -20   Vertical: -15
       Undefined Areas: Repeat Edge Pixels

- Save changes to "Image 2." (⌘S or **File**)
  Combine "Image 1" and "Image 2": Open the Calculations dialog 5
  box. (**Image**)   Source 1: Image 2   Source 2: Image 1
       Blending: Difference   Result: New

- Apply the Auto Levels command. (**Image>Adjust**)
  Invert the image. (⌘I or **Image>Map**) Save as "Image 3." (**File**)

- Combine "Image 1" and "Image 3": Open the Calculations dialog
  box. (**Image**)   Source 1: Image 1   Source 2: Image 3
       Blending: Difference   Result: New

- Invert the image. (⌘I or **Image>Map**)
  Apply the Auto Levels command (**Image>Adjust**)
  Select the Grayscale mode option. (**Mode**)
  Select the CMYK mode option. (**Mode**)
  Open the Hue/Saturation (⌘U or **Image>Adjust**)
       Hue: -100   Saturation: 100   Brightness: 25

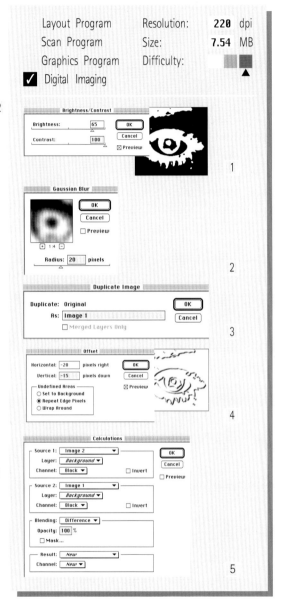

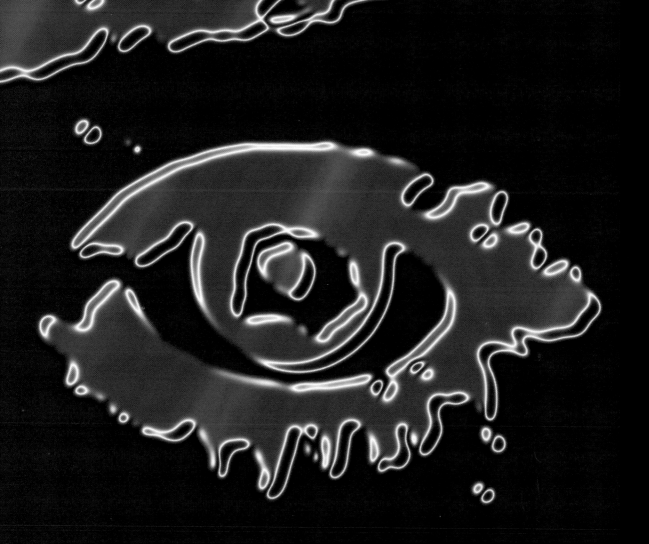

Metal Sign

- Open the original halftone in Photoshop. (⌘**O** or **File**)
  Open the Brightness/Contrast dialog box.
  (⌘**B** or **Image>Adjust**)   Brightness: 60   Contrast: 100
  Apply the Gaussian Blur filter. (**Filter>Blur**)   Radius: 25 pixels 1
  Open the Levels dialog box. (⌘**L** or **Image>Adjust**)
  Increase the black Input Levels, decrease the white Input Levels.

- Select All (⌘**A** or **Select**) and Cut (⌘**X** or **Edit**) the image.
  Open the Channels palette. (**Window>Palettes**) Create a new 2
  Channel. Name it "Metal Mask" Paste the selection from the
  Clipboard. (⌘**V** or **Edit**) Invert the image. (⌘**I** or **Image>Map**)

- Target the Black Channel. (**Channels palette**)
  Apply a Fill. (**Edit**) *Shortcut: Shift & Delete brings up the Fill dialog box.*
     Use: 50% gray   Opacity: 100%   Mode: Normal

- Apply the following filters:
  Add Noise (**Filter>Blur**) Amount: 500   Distribution: Gaussian
  Gaussian Blur (**Filter>Blur**)   Radius: 1 pixels
  Facet (**Filter>Pixelate**)   Blur More (**Filter>Blur**)

- Apply the Auto Levels command. (**Image>Adjust**)
  Apply the Emboss filter (**Filter>Stylize**) 3
     Angle: 135°   Height: 4 pixels   Amount: 100%

- Open the Channels palette. (**Window>Palettes**) Target "Metal Mask."
  Select All (⌘**A** or **Select**) and Copy (⌘**C** or **Edit**) the image.
  Create a new Channel. Name it "Channel 3."
  Paste the selection from the Clipboard. (⌘**V** or **Edit**)
  Apply the Gaussian Blur filter. (**Filter>Blur**)   Radius: 15 pixels
  Apply the Offset filter. (**Filter>Other**) 4
     Horizontal: 40   Vertical: 40
     Undefined Areas: Repeat Edge Pixels

- Target the Black channel. Use the Load Selection command. (**Select**)
  Load "Channel 3." Open the Levels dialog box. (⌘**L** or
  Image>Adjust) Adjust the Input Levels to darken the image.

- Apply the Load Selection command. (**Select**) Load "Metal Mask."
  Use the Airbrush tool to create glare.
  Select the CMYK mode option. (**Mode**)
  Open the Hue/Saturation dialog box. (⌘**U** or **Image>Adjust**) 5
     Hue: 35   Saturation: 100   Lightness: +40

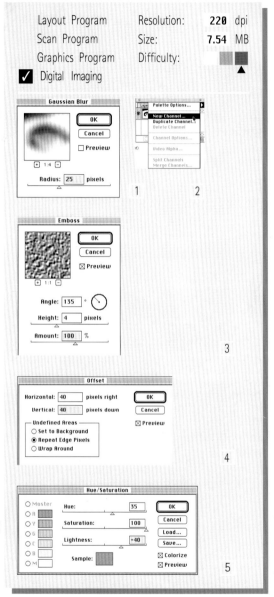

Layout Program
Scan Program
Graphics Program
☑ Digital Imaging

Resolution: **220** dpi
Size: **7.54** MB
Difficulty:

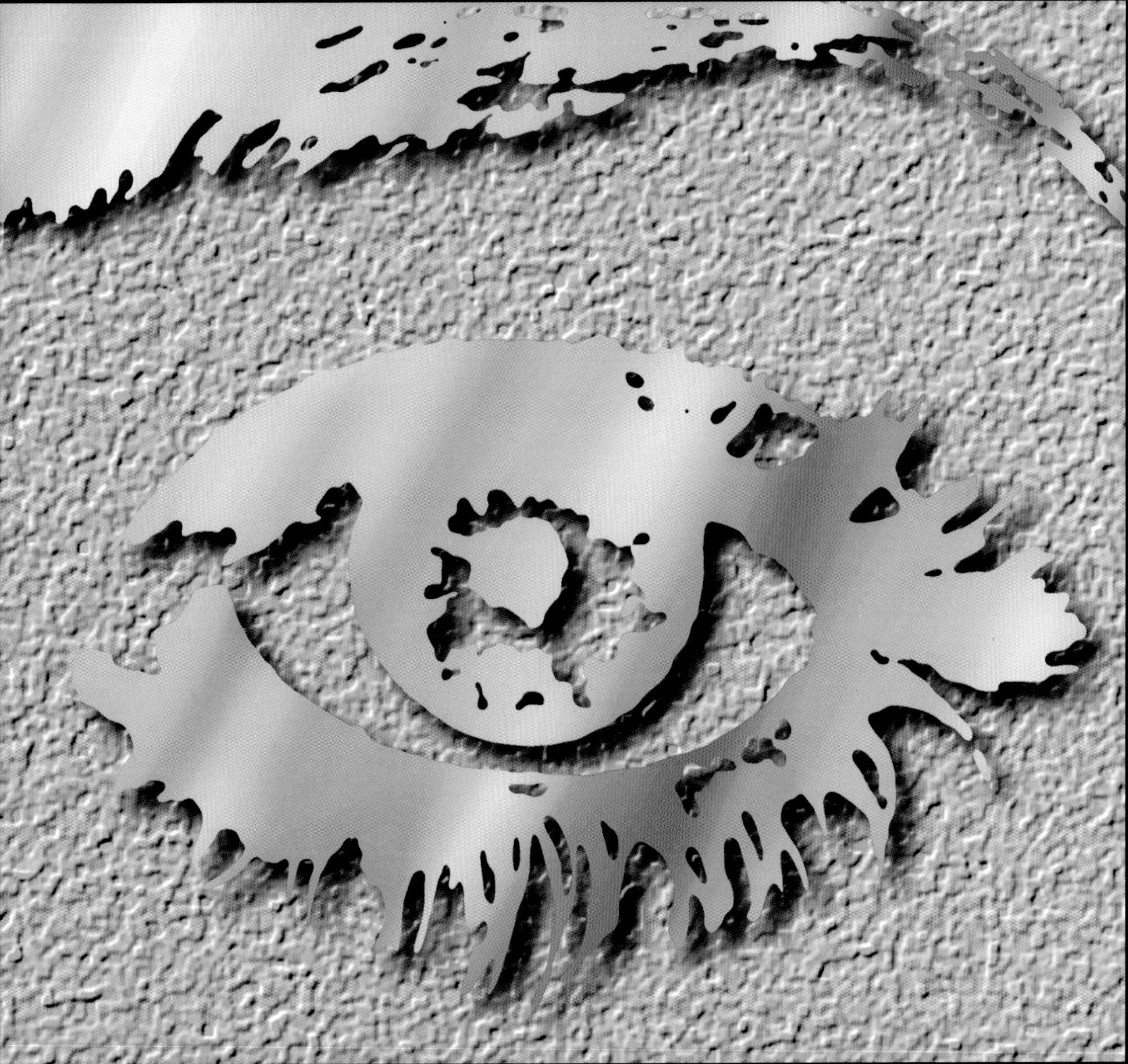

Neon

- Open the original halftone in Photoshop. (**⌘O** or **File**)
  Select the CMYK mode option. (**Mode**)

- Open the Paths palette. (**Window>Palettes**) 1
  Create a new Path. Name it "Neon."

- Trace the image's outline using the Pen.

- Target the Background layer.
  Select All (**⌘A** or **Select**) and Delete.

- Double-click the Airbrush tool. 2
          Paint mode: Normal   Pressure: 100%
  Choose a custom color from the Color Picker.
  Select the 35 pixel soft brush from Brushes palette. 3

- Target the Paths palette. Use the Pointer and click on each
  of the paths. Choose Stroke Paths from the Paths palette menu. 4
          Tool: Airbrush
  Delete the marked paths.

- Target the Channels Palette. Select and Delete the Black channel.

- Invert the image. (**⌘I** or **Image>Map**)

- Select the Grayscale mode option. (**Mode**)
  Select the Indexed Colors mode option. (**Mode**)
  Open the Color Table dialog box. (**Mode**)   Table: Custom
  Select the top four rows of squares. Choose Black as the first
  color and magenta as the last color from the Color Picker.

- Open the Color Table dialog box. (**Mode**)   Table: Custom
  Select the bottom twelve rows of squares. Choose magenta as the
  first color, and white as the last color from the Color Picker.

- Select the CMYK mode option. (**Mode**)
  Open the Layers Palette. Duplicate the Background layer.
  Target the new layer.
  Apply the Gaussian Blur filter. (**Filter>Blur**)   Radius: 40 pixels 5
  Choose Overlay from the Layer Mode pop-up menu. 6

- Open the Levels dialog box. (**⌘L** or **Image>Adjust**)
  Experiment to enhance the tonal ranges of the image.

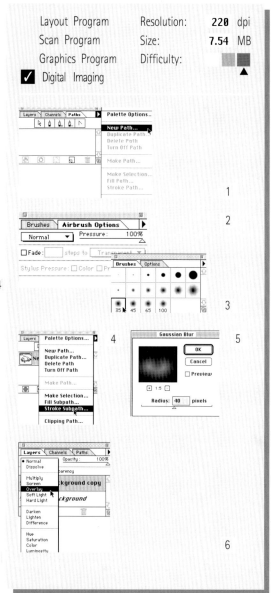

Layout Program	Resolution:	**220**	dpi
Scan Program	Size:	**7.54**	MB
Graphics Program	Difficulty:		
✓ Digital Imaging			

1

2

3

4

5

6

Glass Shards

Layout Program   Resolution: **220** dpi

Scan Program   Size: **6.9** MB

✓ Graphics Program   Difficulty:

Digital Imaging

- Create a New document within FreeHand. (⌘**N** or **File**)

- Generate three new Layers. (**Layers palette**) 1
  Name them "Shards," "Light Edges," and "Bottom."
  Target the layer "Shards."

- With the Pen tool, create an illustration of glass shards. 2
  They must be independently closed shapes.
  Make the file the same size and resolution as the original
  halftone.

- Select All (⌘**A** or **Edit**) and Clone (⌘**=** or **Edit**) the image.
  Place this clone in the layer "Light Edges."

- Select All (⌘**A** or **Edit**) and move the shapes up and to the left.

- Fill the shapes with white. *Drag the white swatch from the
  Color List to the Fill Selector.*

- Fill the layer "Bottom" with a Black background.

- Click off the check marks next to the layers "Bottom" and
  "Light Edges." *This will make them invisible.* 3

- Target the layer "Shards." Place the original image in FreeHand
  as a TIFF. (⌘ **Shift D** or **File**) Align it precisely over the
  entire pattern. Cut the image to the Clipboard. (⌘**X** or **Edit**)

- Select one of the shard shapes.
  Apply the Paste Inside. (⌘ **Shift V** or **Edit**)
  Repeat the Select and Paste Inside procedure with the rest of
  the shapes.

- Select All. (⌘**A** or **Edit**)
  Make the lines transparent by drag the None swatch from the
  Color List to the Stoke Selector. 4

- Click on the check marks next to all the layers to make them visible.

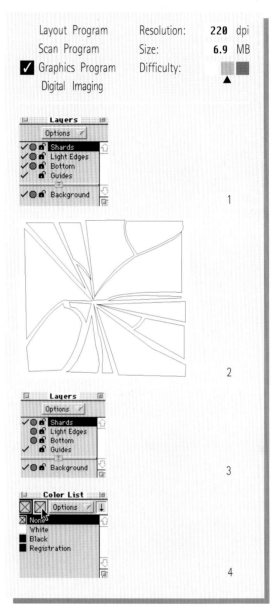

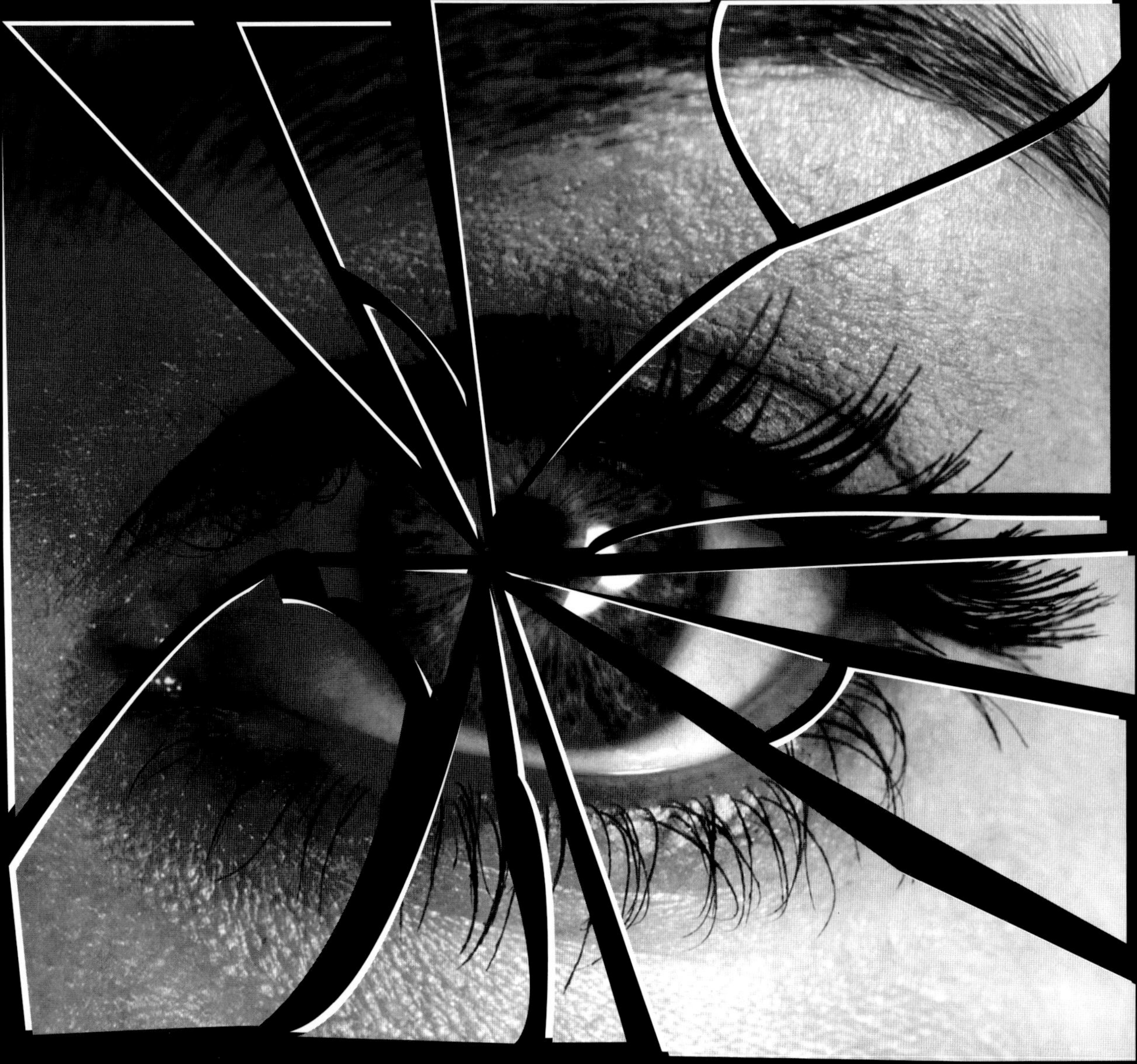

Fire

- Scan an image of fire in RGB mode. Name it "Fire." Make the file the same size and resolution as the original halftone. Open the image "Fire" in Photoshop. (**⌘O** or **File**)

- Select the Indexed Colors mode option. (**Mode**) Open the Color Table dialog box. (**Mode**) Table: Custom 1 Save the table as "Flames."

- Select the RGB mode option. (**Mode**)

- Open the original halftone in Photoshop. (**⌘O** or **File**)

- Select the RGB mode option. (**Mode**) Select the Indexed Colors mode option. (**Mode**) Open the Color Table dialog box. (**Mode**) Load the table "Flames."

- Select the Move tool and drag "Fire" onto the original halftone's document window. A new layer is generated containing the fire image. Name it "Fire."

- Target the layer "Fire." Choose Add Layer Mask from the Layers palette pop-up menu. 2 *The layer mask preview will appear.* Reset your Foreground and Background colors.

- Double-click on the Gradient tool. 3
  Paint mode: Normal   Opacity: 100%
  Style: Foreground to Background
  Midpoint Skew: 50%
  Type: Linear   Check Dither.
  Create a vertical gradient by dragging from the top of the image to the bottom.

- To apply the mask permanently, choose Remove Layer Mask from the Layers palette pop-up menu. Click Apply.

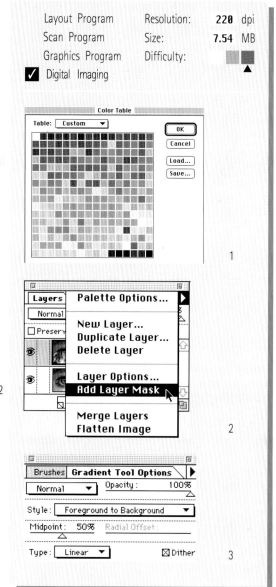

Layout Program   Resolution: **220** dpi
Scan Program   Size: **7.54** MB
Graphics Program Difficulty:
✓ Digital Imaging

Cartoon

- Open the original halftone in FreeHand as a TIFF. (⌘O or **File**)

- Place the image onto the Background layers:
  Open the Layers palette.
  Select the image and double-click on the Background layer.

- Target the Foreground layer.
  Roughly trace the various shapes with the Pen tool.
  They must be independently closed shapes.

- Fill the shapes with color:
  Choose a color from the Color Mixer and drag the swatch to
  the Color List.   1
  Then drag the color swatch from the Color List to the Fill
  Selector or to the image. Repeat for all the shapes.

- Color the lines black:
  Drag the black swatch from the Color List to the Stoke
  Selector.

- Create a drop-shadow effect:
  Select All (⌘A or **Edit**) and Clone (⌘= or **Edit**) the image.
  Drag the shapes down and to the right.

- Fill the shapes with black.
  Drag the black swatch from the Color List to the Fill Selector.
  Apply the Send to Back command. (⌘B or **Arrange**)
  This shuffles the drop shadow behind the colored shapes.

- Target the Background image.
  Select and delete the original image.
  Draw a rectangle for a background surface.

- Fill the rectanglewith green:
  Choose a shade of green from the Color Mixer.   2
  Drag the swatch to the Color List.
  Then drag the color swatch from the Color List to the Fill
  Selector or to the object itself.

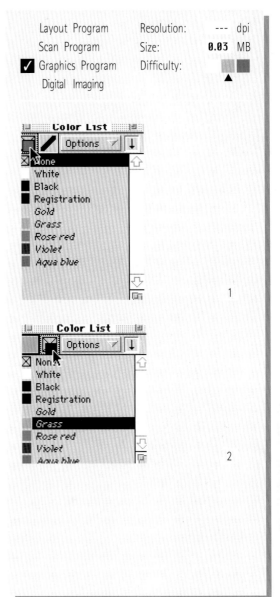

Layout Program
Scan Program
✓ Graphics Program
Digital Imaging

Resolution: --- dpi
Size: **0.03** MB
Difficulty:

1

2

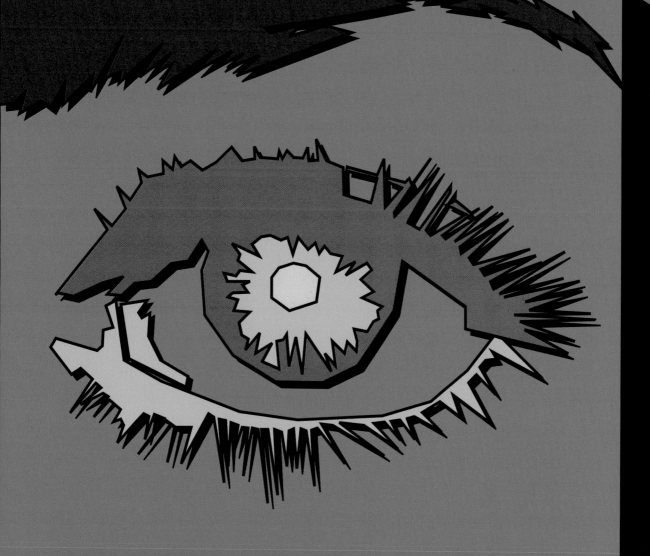

Abstract Sketching

Layout Program   Resolution: **220** dpi
Scan Program   Size: **2.6** MB
☑ Graphics Program   Difficulty:
Digital Imaging

- Open the original halftone in FreeHand as a TIFF.
  (⌘**O** or **File**)

- Give the image a 40% tint:
  Choose 40% gray from the Color Mixer.
  Drag the swatch to the Color List.
  Then drag the color swatch from the Color List to the Fill
  Selector or to the image. 1

- Open the Layers palette.
  Move the image onto the Background layers:
  Select the image, then double-click on the Background
  layer.

- Activate the Foreground layer.
  Create abstract drawings and place them over the eye.
  *Use creative license here. Explore various lines and shapes
  with various colors, gradients and patterns.*

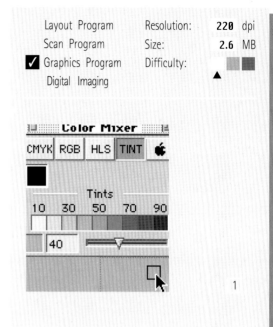

1

4

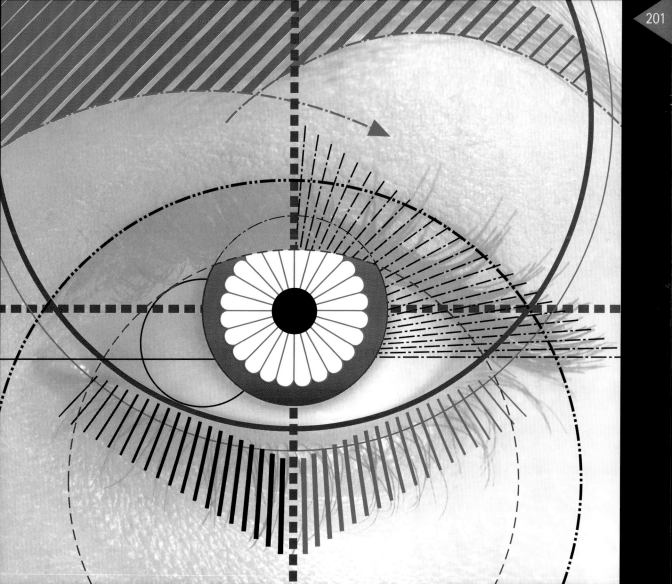

Clouds

Layout Program	Resolution:	**220** dpi
Scan Program	Size:	**7.54** MB
Graphics Program	Difficulty:	
✓ Digital Imaging		▲

- Scan an image of clouds in black and white. Name it "Clouds." Make sure this file is the same size and resolution as the original halftone.
  Open the scan in Photoshop. (⌘O or **File**)

- Open the original halftone in Photoshop. (⌘O or **File**)
  Drag the layer from the Layer palette to the image "Clouds." A new layer is formed with your original image in it.

- Target the layer containing the original image.
  Choose Add Layer Mask from the Layers palette pop-up menu. *The layer mask preview will appear.*

- Double-click the Lasso tool.　1
  　　Feather: 20 pixels　　　　Check Anti-aliased.
  Select an area to be masked.

- Inverse the selection. (**Select**)

- Apply a Fill. (**Edit**)　2
  Shortcut: Shift & Delete keys bring up the Fill dialog box.
  　　Use: Black　　　Opacity: 100%　　Mode: Normal

- Apply the None command. (⌘D or **Select**)
  This ensures nothing is selected.

- Make black your Foreground color.
  Shortcut: the D key sets the colors back to default.

- Double-click the Airbrush tool.　3
  　　Paint mode: Normal　　　Pressure: 50
  Select a 65 pixel soft brush.　4
  Use the Airbrush to add to the mask. If you need to subtract 5 from the mask, choose white as your foreground color, and paint away the mask.

- Select the CMYK mode option. (**Mode**)
  Open the Hue/Saturation dialog box. (⌘U or **Image>Adjust**)
  　　Hue: -155　　　Saturation: 70　　　Lightness: 0

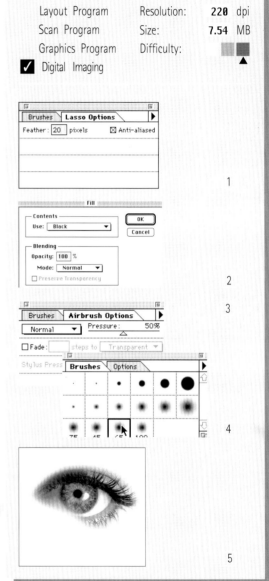

1

2

3

4

5

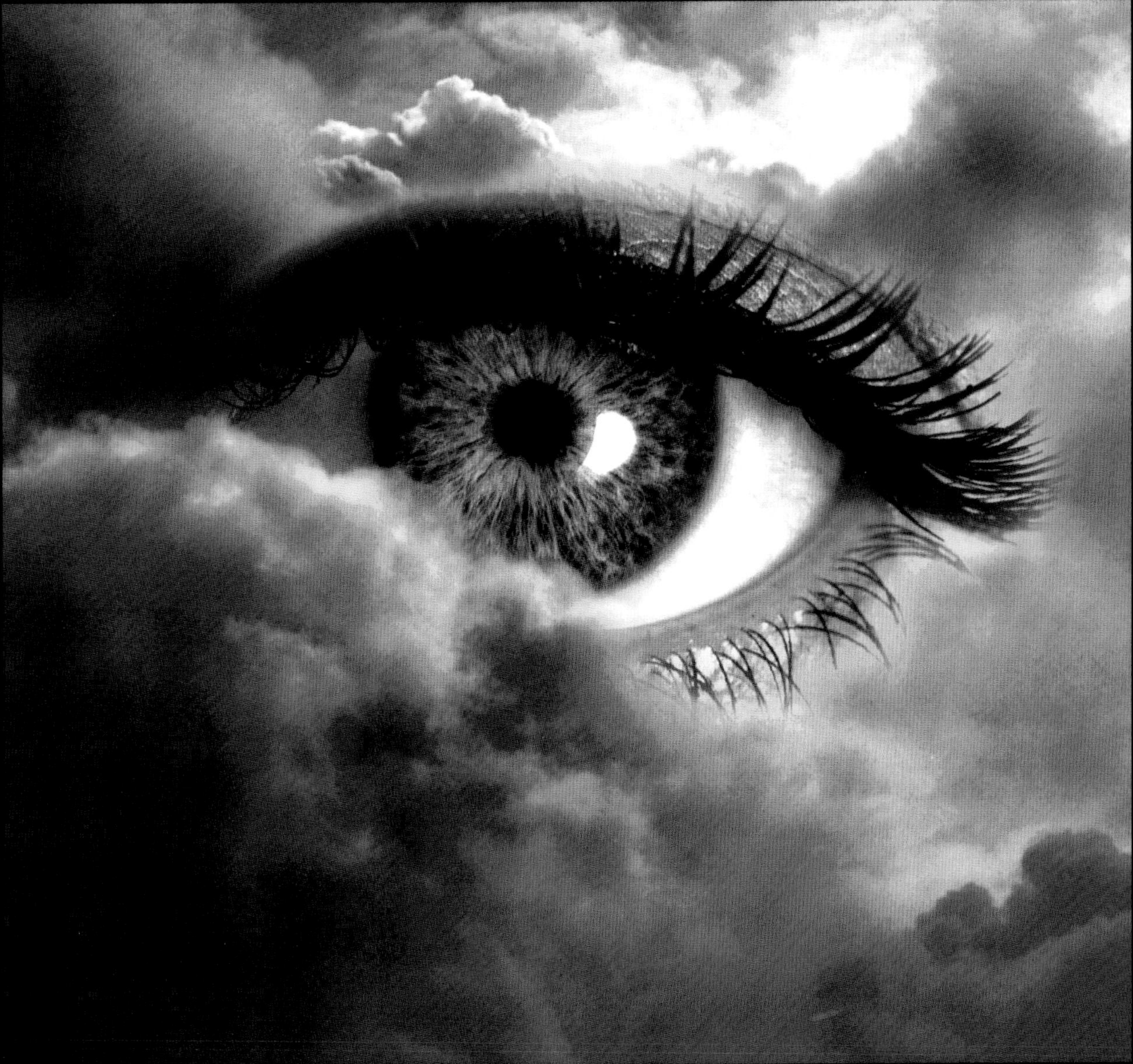

Color Swash *(Cover Photo)*

- Scan an image of a brush stroke in black and white. Name it "Swash." Make the file the same size and resolution as the original halftone. Open the scan in Photoshop. (⌘0 or **File**)

- Open the original halftone in Photoshop. (⌘0 or **File**)
  Apply the Mosaic filter. (**Filter>Pixelate**) 1
      Cell Size: 35 pixels square
  Select the CMYK mode option. (**Mode**)
  Save the file as "Mosaic." (**Edit**)

- Activate the file "Swash."
  Double-click the Magic Wand tool.   Tolerance: 0 2
  Use the Magic Wand tool to select the black brush stroke.
  Drag the selection to the file "Mosaic."
  Turn the selection into a layer: Open the layers palette.
  Double-click on "Floating Selection." *This brings up the Make Layer dialog box.* Name the layer "Swash."

- Open the original halftone in Photoshop. (⌘0 or **File**)
  Select the RGB mode option. (**Mode**)
  Select the Indexed Colors mode option. (**Mode**)
  Open the Color Table dialog box. (**Mode**)   Table: Spectrum
  Select the CMYK mode option. (**Mode**)

- Drag this layer from the layer palette to the file "Mosaic." 3
  A new layer is formed with your original image in it.
  Double-click on it. *The Layer Options dialog box appears.*
  Name it "Original."

- Create a Clipping Group: Double-click on your original image layer to open the Layers Options dialog box. 4
  Click on the Group With Previous Layer box.

- Target the layer "Swash." Choose Duplicate Layer from the Layers palette menu. *Shortcut: Drag the layer thumbnail onto the New Layer icon.*

- Target the layer "Swash." Choose the Move tool.
  Click on the image and drag it slightly down and to the right to create a drop-shadow effect. *The arrow keys can also be used to position it.*

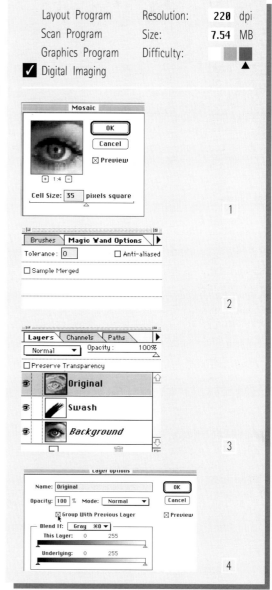

Layout Program	Resolution:	220	dpi
Scan Program	Size:	7.54	MB
Graphics Program	Difficulty:		
✓ Digital Imaging			

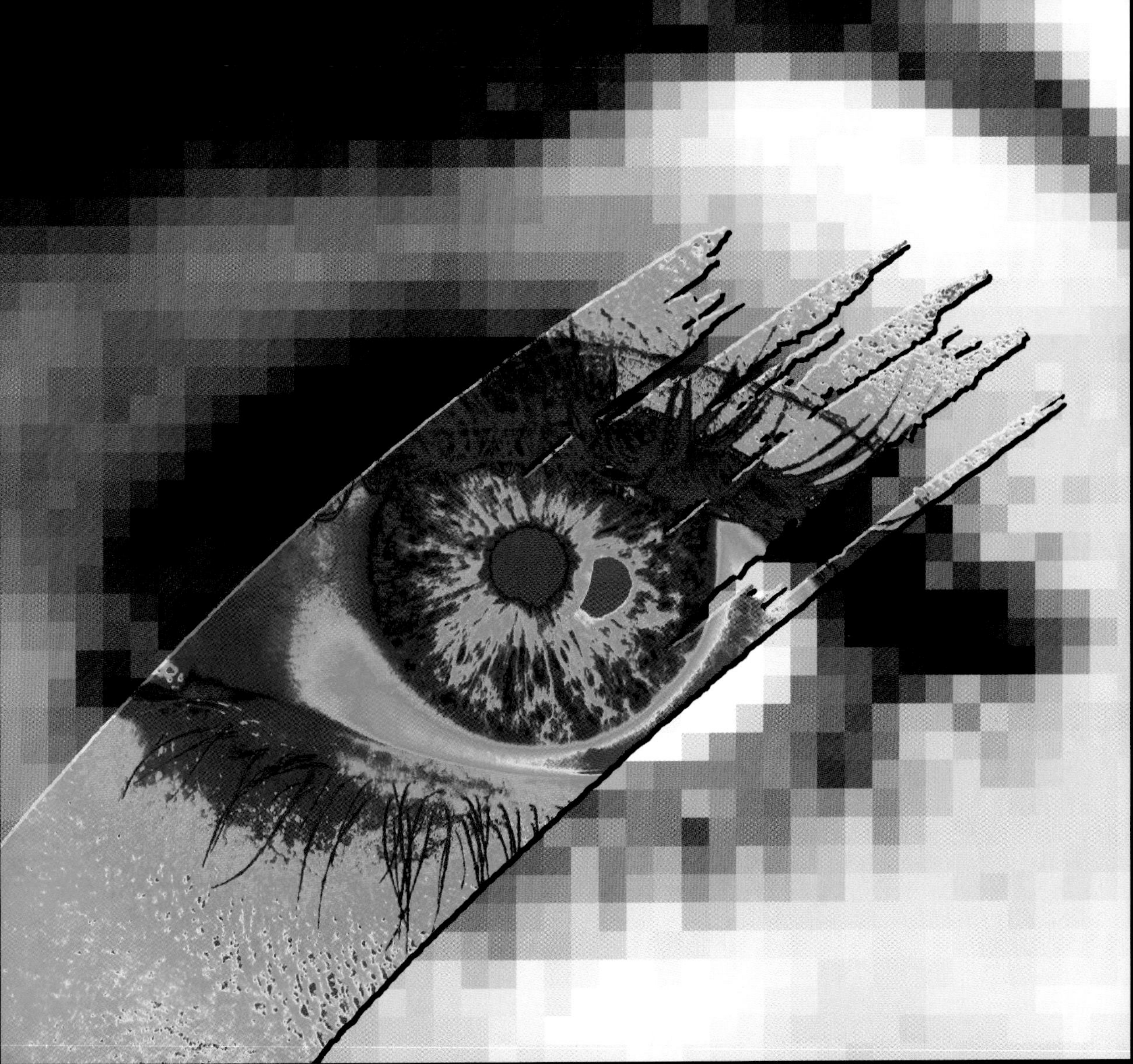